Uh-oh! I thought you might like this - don't know why?

Happy Christmas Reading !!

lots of love

...who?

THE PRIVATE EYE ANNUAL 2000

EDITED BY IAN HISLOP

Published in Great Britain by
Private Eye Productions Ltd
6 Carlisle Street, London W1D 5BN

© 2000 Pressdram Ltd
ISBN 1 901784 215
Designed by Bridget Tisdall
Printed in England by
Ebenezer Baylis & Son Ltd, Worcester

2 4 6 8 10 9 7 5 3 1

THE PRIVATE EYE ANNUAL 2000

EDITED BY IAN HISLOP

"Run – it's the Philistines!"

PRIVATE EYE CELEBRATES ITS FIRST 1000 YEARS

FOR the last millennium Private Eye has taken a wry sideways look at the news as and when it happened. From King Harold to Harold Wilson, from Bonnie Prince Charlie to Boring Prince Charlie, the Domesday Book to the Dome, Private Eye has tickled the nation's funnybone through war, famine, plague and death. Here at last are the classic covers from ten centuries of historical hilarity – for you to cut out and keep in your wastepaper bin.

PRIVATE EYE

THE BATTLE OF MAX HASTINGS!

This'll get you in the Eye, Harold!

1066

PRIVATE EYE

IT'S PETER MAGNA CARTA RUCK!

Sign here or we issue writs!

1215

PRIVATE EYE

AGINCOURT
YES, IT'S THE HUNDRED YEARS BORE!

Don'tcha just love the Archers?

1413

PRIVATE EYE

ARMADA: TASK FORCE GOES IN

Rejoice, Rejoice!

1588

PRIVATE EYE

MONARCHY TO BE AXED

That's enough, head

1649

PRIVATE EYE

LONDON GOES SHARE CRAZY!

That's the South Sea Bubble

1720

PRIVATE EYE

WELLINGTON PUTS BOOT IN

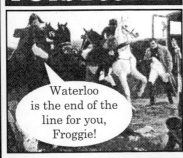

Waterloo is the end of the line for you, Froggie!

1815

PRIVATE EYE

JOHN BROWN WINDSOR SCOOP!

We are not amused!

1880

PRIVATE EYE

OSCAR TRIUMPH!

Bugger me, I've been arrested!

1895

MILLIONS OF SPIES REVEALED

Defector's Shocking List Of Traitors

by Our Espionage Staff **Jack Tinker** and **A.J.P. Taylor-Soldier-Spy**

IN THE most sensational revelation ever to be revealed, Soviet defector Boris Jonsonov, Chief Librarian of the KGB Secret Central Archive, has revealed the names of millions of top-ranking British spies who between them nearly brought about the total collapse of Western civilisation as we know it.

Top of the list is Mrs Ethel Prunehat, 87, possibly the most dangerous KGB agent this country has ever known.

As a junior employee in the ball-bearing manufacturing company of Wibblings and Wapps of Neasden, Mrs Prunehat had access to the most sensitive ball-bearing related information which at the time could have helped Soviet scientists develop the first atomic-powered rollerblade.

Also named in Jonsonov's earth-shattering dossier are Sir Anthony Blunt, Burgess, McLean and Philby (the so-called "Secret Seven"), Dr No and Rosa Klebb who *(cont'd. p. 94)*

ON OTHER PAGES

☐ How the KGB planned to put a whoopee cushion on Prince Charles's Investiture Throne and thus destabilise the Monarchy by CHAPMAN PINCHYERMATERIAL **2**

☐ Why Mrs Prunehat, the greatest traitor since Guy Fawkes, should swing by historian *(Shurely shome mishtake? Ed.)* ANDREW ROBERTS **3**

☐ More stuff you knew already by EVERYONE ELSE **4-94**

Eye Readers Choose Their 100 Favourite TV Moments

1 1992. Shaznee leaves Dwayne for Terry in *Neighbours*.

2 1996. Sid Moron tells Alan Titchmarsh to "F*** off" on controversial breakfast TV show.

3 1998. The famous "Armadillo gets diarrhoea" episode in popular BBC series *The Paravets*.

4 1993. Des Lynam's moustache catches fire in *Match Of The Day* studio.

5 1991. England vs. The Vatican. Gary Knobbs scores treble hat-trick in extra time as England fail to beat Pontiffs XI.

6 1996. The famous blocked toilet scene from *Birds Of A Feather*" (series 8).

7 1953. James Chuter-Ede crashes out in Newport Pagnell by-election, signalling end of twenty years of *(Shurely shome mishtake? Ed.)*

- PUBROW -

Calling Moscow... I think I've got away with it... Over.

SPY WHO CAME IN FROM THE OLD

TEN TELL-TALE SIGNS THAT MI5 MISSED IN THE NEASDEN MATA HARI

1. She was chairman of the Neasden Women's Institute for the Overthrow of Capitalism.
2. She organised regular trips for the Darby and Joan Club to have tea and scones with senior KGB figures.
3. She listed her hobbies in "Who's Who" as spying for the KGB.
4. She had a life-size statue of Stalin in her front garden.
5. Her cottage in Wirral Lane, Neasden, was known to locals as "The Lubyanka".
6. When watching James Bond films in the Neasden Roxy she always booed when 007 appeared.
7. Er...
8. That's enough tell-tale signs.

CAUGHT AND CIRCULATED

KENSINGTON PALACE

Saturday. Lord Frederick Windsor, the 94th in line to the line of cocaine, will today attend a party at which he will go to the toilets and be attended by Rupert Snortington-Spoone (O.E.). Lord Frederick will be offered a small quantity of high quality Colombian cocained mixed with talcum powder, bleach and granulated sugar, which he will graciously purchase from Mr Spoone for the sum of £500.

He will then return to the party talking excitedly in a loud voice about "Charlie".

Mr Spoone will proceed to a phone box from where he will contact a Mr Les Filth from the *News of the World* and inform him about Lord Frederick's recent transaction.

BUCKINGHAM PALACE

Sunday. Prince Edward, the Earl of Wessex, will read the story about Lord Frederick Windsor in the *News of the World* with extreme pleasure, since the headline "What A Right Royal Twit" will not, for once, apply to himself.

From the best-selling author of Born To Be Queen, Heir of Sorrows *and* La Dame Aux Camillas, *now comes the greatest love story of them all.*

Never Too Old...

by Dame Sylvie Krin

THE STORY SO FAR: Billionaire media-mogul Rupert Murdoch has at last discovered true love in the twilight years of his life. Now read on...

"Grunt. Grunt. Grunt."
"Keep going, darling."
"This is going to kill me!"
"Is it, darling? Ha, ha, ha, ha!"

THE SWEATING septuagenarian pulled one more time at the oars of the Kami Kazi indoor rowing machine, and then slumped forward.

His svelte young Oriental bride rushed forward eagerly, with a glass of Chinese herbal viagra made by Buddhist monks in the mountains of Hah-don province.

She helped the exhausted press baron to his feet and guided him to his favourite rocking chair, looking down from the 58th floor onto the sparkling wavelets of the Rock Hudson River.

"Blimey, Wendy, I'm pooped. I'm sweating worse than an abo's armpit. But I reckon I've lost at least eight pounds in the past two hours."

His young wife's inscrutable porcelain features registered a moment of alarm.

"Not too many pounds, I hope, honeybun!" she exclaimed. "That's not my idea at all."

Rupert took a swig of his oriental love potion, before replying: "This stuff's certainly given me a bit of an idea, Wend. And this isn't a kangaroo's tail you're looking at!"

As if to echo the mogul's inmost thoughts, the tugs on the river below all hooted in raunchy unison.

"No time for that now, you dirty old digger," mocked the bewitching siren from the land of bird's nest soup. "You've got to get dressed for our photo-shoot with *Vanity Fair.*"

"**V**ANITY FAIR," announced the disembodied voice from the intercom 300 floors below. "We've come for the interview."

"Come on up, we're ready," breathed the shapely temptress from the land of shark's fin noodles.

An hour later, Stothard the butler announced: "Mr William Shawcross, the official biographer, is here, milady, accompanied by a number of gentlemen with photographic devices."

The young Mrs Murdoch immediately took charge.

"Let's forget about the words. You can make them up later, Mr Shawcross."

"Very good, madam," replied the obsequious litterateur, "I'll send them along later for your approval, as usual."

"Just make sure you get the clothes right," she added, in an imperious tone. "Ru-pert!"

From the master bedroom emerged the scarcely recognisable figure of the world's most powerful media tycoon.

Despite his 87 years, he was clad from head to foot in the latest designer clothes from the world's leading couturiers.

"Walk up and down, dear, and try not to fall over," she ordered.

The owner of 20th Century Fox and the Times Newspaper Group of London, England, shuffled forward, as if on a catwalk, while his partner intoned "Rupert is wearing a soot-black three-ply cashmere turtle-neck from the House of Ziggy Mitsubushi. Note how discreetly it complements the stone-washed brushed denim loose-fit combat trousers from Tommy Fingerfood of Boston. And don't forget the shoes."

She broke off, as she noticed in horror that her beloved billionaire husband had forgotten to put on the Yelland and Mackenzie all-weather deck shoes she had carefully chosen, and had instead donned a pair of well-worn Marks & Spencer's tartan bedroom slippers.

"Stop!" she barked. "The whole thing's a disaster. You can only photograph him from the knees up..."

"**K**NEES UP! Arms up! Come on, Rupert, you've got another 200 press-ups before you're allowed your frozen soya drink!"

"Jeez," wheezed the panting press lord, as he struggled to get through the new Chinese Air Force "Get Fit Or Die" exercise regime. "This will finish me off."

The sultry sex goddess from Szechuan allowed an enigmatic smile to play around her rose-petal mouth...

To be continued

MUMMY, WHY ARE YOUR HANDS SO SOFT?

I'M TWELVE

Radio Highlights

Radio 4

The Today Programme

John Humphrys: I have with me in the studio the author of a controversial new book about declining standards in our society. John, this is just a load of old reactionary nonsense, isn't it?

John Humphrys *(for it is he)*: What I was trying to do in my book was point out...

John Humphrys: Come off it, John, this is just a rabid rant from an old-timer on the way out, isn't it?

John Humphrys: It seems to me that in Britain today...

John Humphrys: Well, is it rubbish or isn't it?

John Humphrys: I don't think that I can...

John Humphrys: Yes or no?

John Humphrys: It is not fair to...

John Humphrys: Yes or no, John?

John Humphrys: You've asked that question five times now, John...

John Humphrys: Then give me an answer, you old... *(Cont'd. 94 MHz)*

PORTILLO'S SECRET SHAME: "YES, I WAS A TORY"

by Our Political Staff Gay Search

MICHAEL PORTILLO, the well-known homosexual TV personality, has admitted that as a young man he was "a friend of Maggie".

He told the Times newspaper, "Like a lot of young men, I swung to the right and belonged to a group of pretty outrageous Tories.

"However, I have now come out of the cabinet and I have put all that youthful indiscretion behind me.

"I am now a compassionate, caring, liberal, middle-of-the-road politician."

MICHAEL! MICHAEL! MICHAEL! OUT! OUT! OUT!

When challenged about the level of his involvement with the seedy practices of "Tories" in the 1980s, Portillo admitted:

"Look, I don't want to go into detail, but there was a certain amount of licking bottoms, screwing large numbers of working men, and generally buggering up the country."

Mr Portillo made an impassioned plea for people not to hold his shameful past against him.

"Please concentrate on my private affairs," he said, "and don't judge me on my public life."

William Hague is finished.

AN ALTERNATIVE VOICE
CEDRIC SPART

THE nauseating hypocrisy of Michael Portillo is totally nauseating, ie his admission that he was gay in the past, but is now a straight, which is highly offensive to all members of the gay and lesbian community because, as we all know, anyone who has been gay must always be gay, even if they pretend for reasons of social hypocrisy to revert to a heterosexual life-style, er, not only that but Portillo has gone on record as voting against gays in the military and against lowering the age of consent, which proves conclusively that he is gay, er, surely Peter Tatchell is right when he says (cont'd. p. 94)

St Cakes

Peterhouse term begins today. There are 210 gays in the school and 2 straights. R.J.L. Pinke-Trouser (Portillo's) is Head Sailor. P.J.B. Youthful-Fumbling (Driberg's) is Keeper of the Cottage. Rev. P.D. O'Phile has left to take over the chaplaincy of St Kincora's Home in North Wales. His place is taken by The Very Rev. D.C. Pocket-Billiard (formerly Chaplain to the Admiralty). There will be a performance of "The Buggers Opera" by John Gay on Nov. 3rd in the Lower Passage. Sir Ian Mackellan (O.C.) will open the new toilet block on Founders Day. Outings are on Dec. 12th.

THE DAILY TELEGRAPH

Octogenarian Surrogate Mum Gives Birth To Piglets For Gay Couple

By Our Medical Breakthrough Staff Dr Frank N. Stein

IN WHAT was described as "the most important medical breakthrough of all time," an 87-year-old Norfolk woman yesterday gave birth to *(cont'd. p. 94)*

THE TOP 100 BRITISH FILMS OF ALL TIME

(continued from p. 49)

No. 97 THEY FLEW TO BRUGES (1953). David Lean's black-and-white WWII classic tells the story of the ill-fated RAF mission to Bruges, starring Donald Sinden, John Mills and Richard Attenborough as "Sparks".

No. 98 BLOKE (1973). Ken Loach's harrowing masterpiece about a young unemployed Northerner who befriends a stray ferret, before being run over by a rich local slum landlord.

No. 99 THE NEASDEN THUNDERBOLT (1951). Boulting Brothers' good-humoured satire on the state of the railway industry in post-war Britain. Cameo role for young George Cole as the station-master's assistant.

No. 100 CARRY ON GOING TO THE TOILET (1964).

(That's enough films. Ed.)

THE DAILY TELEGRAPH

Letters to the Editor
Gays In The Services

SIR — I fail to see what all the fuss is about. In my day, it was well known that many officers, not to say other ranks, were what we used to call "Billy Bothways". Their identities and proclivities were an open secret, and what they got up to in the privacy of their own latrines was entirely their own business. However, when it came to the field of battle, these chaps proved that they were every bit as brave as the average red-blooded Tommy Atkins.

BRIG. J.F.Q. FARQUHARSON-GUSSETT,
Tatchell St Peter, Beds

SIR — Those of us who are familiar with Thucydides' account of the Peloponnesian War will recall that, at the Battle of Homophobia in 426 BC, the Spartans relied for their victory on a regiment of highly-trained homosexuals, known as the *sodomitides*. Although only 40 strong, they defeated an Athenian army of 40,000 men, thus earning themselves immortality.

PROF. SHIRLEY BASSEY
The Judy Garland Chair of Classical Studies,
University of Soho
(formerly Doc Johnson's Love Shop)

GREAT STATESMAN DIES

A Nation Mourns

by **Our Entire Staff**

ONE OF the towering figures of post-war British politics has died.

Tributes flowed in from all over the country at the news that the greatest Conservative thinker of his generation had died at his castle on the cliffs of his beloved Kent.

But "Alan", as he was known to his millions of admirers throughout the civilised world, was not just a mere politician.

His diaries were possibly the greatest contribution to confessional literature since Pepys.

And he was not just a politician and a diarist. He was arguably the greatest war historian of all time.

His masterpiece "Why We Should Have Joined Up With Hitler Instead Of That Creep Stalin" changed conventional thinking about World War Two forever.

And he was not just a politician, a diarist and an historian.

He was also one of the greatest drivers of fast cars of all time.

And he was not just a driver of fast *(continued for 94 more pages)*

ON OTHER PAGES

● Was My Friend Alan The Greatest Prime Minister We Never Had? *asks Paul Johnson*
● Why I Blubbed When I Heard The News *by Boo-hoo-hoos Anderson*
● Why We Will Never See His Like Again *by Everyone Else*

The Alan I Knew

by TV's Charles Moore

I WELL remember taking Alan out to lunch at the Savoy Grill when he'd just been made Minister for Paperclips. I had ordered a tolerably good bottle of claret, but Alan would have none of it.

"Don't offer me that gnat's piss," he said. "I'm sure Conrad (Lord Black, proprietor of the *Daily Telegraph*) can run to some Chateau Lafite '61." This cost £850, but Alan laughed when I remonstrated with him. "Don't be such a spastic little poofter," he mocked, while giving the coloured waitress a playful grope.

Say what you like about Alan. He may have been a shit, a fascist and a sex-crazed lunatic, but he was very rich and went to Eton.

© *World Copyright, Mooretrash Productions.*

The Wit And Wisdom Of The Great Statesman

On Leadership

"Hitler? Good man."

"Mrs Thatcher? Phwoar, I'd give her one."

On Africa

"Niggy-noggyland, I call it."

"Mmmm, black girls have got marvellous arses."

On History

"Churchill was a leftie who lost us the war."

"Hitler, good egg."

On Europe

"German women, bloody good in the sack."

"Swedish birds, phwoar. Wouldn't you?"

"Hitler, first-rate chap."

On His Parliamentary Colleagues

"Kenneth Clarke. A fat, idle slug."

"Michael Heseltine, a common little spiv who had to buy his own hairbrushes."

"Tom King. A fat, idle slug."

"Clare Short. As Trots go, she is pretty f***able."

On Civil Servants

"Devious, scheming bastards."

On His Rottweilers "Goering" and "Himmler"

"Unlike human beings, they never let me down."

On His Wife Jane

"Not very often."

On Hitler

That's enough wit and wisdom. Ed.

GLENDA SLAGG

Menopause Behaving Badly (geddit!?!)

HATS and everything else off to Charlie Dimmock – gardening's Lady Godiva!?!

A gal who's not ashamed to show off her prize melons!?! "Cor, what a lovely pear!" said one of my colleagues when he saw the photos!?!? "I'd like to have those in my bed for a bit of mulching." *(That's enough filth. Ed.)*

TV'S CHARLIE DIMMOCK – what a slapper!?!? So, the Gormless Gardener has decided to get her tips out for the lads!?! You're not going to win any prizes there, darling!? Even if you apply the Miracle-Gro™!?!

Take a tip from Auntie Glenda, spend your ill-gotten gains from the nudie pix on a decent bra! And throw yourself on the compost heap where you belong!?!?

HERE THEY ARE — Glenda's Favourite Fellas!?!?

● **BILL GATES** – Mmmm! It's not your money I'm after Bill – hang on a minute, yes it is!?!?!

● **BORIS JOHNSON** – Can I be a Spectator when you put your paper to bed?!?!

● **KARL MARX** – OK, so he was a drunk, bearded anti-semitic lunatic!? He knew how to give a gal a kapital night out!?!?! Geddit??!?!

Auf Wheenersehen!?!

"Fresh... natural... organic... d'you think we're made of money?"

POLLY FILLER interviews

NICHOLAS COLERIDGE
Managing Director of Conde Naste

HE'S GOT it all. A lovely tan, perfect teeth, a gorgeous wife, four delightful children, a beautiful house and a brilliant career as glamorous supremo of the world's best and glossiest fashion magazines. But I was determined to get beneath this perfect façade.

My first question was a tough one. "Can I have a job please, Nicholas?"

Coleridge laughs in his charming Old Etonian, best-selling way. "Ha ha ha ha!" he soothes. "My new book is a thriller set in the world of glossy magazines..."

But I am not going to let him off the hook so easily. I continue to probe him mercilessly.

"But surely there is a vacancy for a hard-working, talented female columnist who needs a well-paid post somewhere in your empire?"

Coleridge's notoriously good manners do not fail him.

"My book is not at all autobiographical," he replies. "It's not a roman-à-clef as such – more of a fictional soufflé, a literary trifle, a..."

"*Vogue* would be good," I interrupt him, determined to get the interview back on course, "or *Tatler*. Or *World of Interiors*. I'm not fussy. Would you like to see my CV?"

I hand him a neatly printed sheet which includes full details of all my qualifications.

HIS smile lights up the room and he is clearly impressed by my 11 'O' Levels (including General Studies), 3 'A' Levels, 2:1 in Art, History and Anthropology and journalistic experience dating back to my time as chief sub-editor on *Snog* magazine.

Ever the gentleman, Coleridge neatly places my CV in the bin, adjusting the exquisite cuffs on his Turnbull & Asser shirt as he does so.

"It's been marvellous meeting you," he says, "but I've got another twenty interviews to do this morning, so if we're all finished..."

"Just one last question," I tell him, ambushing him as he shows me the door. "When do I start?"
© *All journalists in all newspapers*

MAJOR SHOCK

I will not be airbrushed out of history

THE ALTERNATIVE VOICE

Dave Spart at the Last Night of the Proms

ONCE again we have been treated to a nauseating display of imperialist, chauvinist, nationalist, neo-fascist flag-waving and chanting, ie the so-called Last Night of the Proms, which it isn't because there will be another equally nauseating display next year by an all-white, all-male, all middle-class elite er... where in the multi-cultural society which is Britain today are the classical Afro-Asian composers such as er and er... er... only the outdated anthems of discredited imperialist dictatorship were heard typified by the archetypal fascist William Blake... *(Cont.'d p. 94)*

David Spart is co-chair of the Guardian Letter Writers Cooperative Society

"Right, Mr Johnson – now say AHHHHH"

The Secret DIARY OF JOHN MAJOR (now aged 56¾)

Monday

The big day has come and my best-selling book *John Major – The Years Of Not Inconsiderable Achievement* has been published. We have cleverly timed it to coincide with the party conference, so that instead of going on about Mrs Thatcher as usual, everyone will be talking about me.

My original thought was that I should go up to Blackpool to make a dramatic appearance on the platform in front of thousands of delegates. However, I realised that this would be in no small measure unfair to Mr Hague, since I would obviously get a standing ovation lasting for many minutes, which would make things very difficult for my successor (not that he has had very much success! That is incidentally the type of brilliant joke you will find in my book, which is now available in all leading booksellers published by Fishwick and Jackson for only £29.99).

Tuesday

The phone rings. It is the Times. "I suppose you want to interview me about my brilliant new book which is now available in all leading booksellers." "Oh no," they said, "we want to ask you whether you have any comment on Lord Norma Lamont's story about how he had to lock you in a cupboard to stop you devaluing the pound?" "I have never heard anything so outrageous in my whole life," I replied. "I have not got time to pass comment on some dreary book written by a clapped-out politician which no one is going to buy."

"You shouldn't be so hard on yourself," said my wife Norman, who had just come into the room and totally missed the point as per usual.

Wednesday

Mr Fishwick has organised a non-stop high-profile promotional tour for me, starting with a ten-minute interview on Radio Cotswold's top breakfast show "Good Morning Cirencester".

It was a long journey, which was not made any better in my judgement by having to read the front page of the Daily Telegraph which carried the headline "She's Back – Tories Welcome Hague's Predecessor With Two-Hour Ovation".

The interview did not begin well, as the young presenter said "We had your brother Terry on once, he was really good. We tried to get your long-lost sister to come on with you this morning, but we couldn't get her number. Pity, because it would have made a great human interest story, the way you pretended that you'd never heard of her."

When I remonstrated with him, and told him to ask me about the book, he said "What book? Do you mean Lord Lamont's?" Then he very rudely put on a record, thanked me for coming in and

told me to take care, which in my judgement is no way to treat a former prime minister of England who has met many famous people including Mr Gorbachev and Cyril Washbrook.

Thursday

The Guardian rang up at 8 o'clock, while I was finishing my bowl of Golden Grahams (which are very superior to Honey Nut Loops in my judgement). "I expect you want to interview me about my best-selling book," I said. "Well, no, actually," replied the young lady journalist. "It's about your O-Levels. The headmaster of your old school has just told us that you never got any. But, according to the cuttings, you claim to have two. Who's telling the truth?"

"I have never heard anything so outrageous," I told her, "since I was accused of being locked in a cupboard by Mr Lamont. I haven't got time to drag

up events from the past which no one is interested in," and put down the phone.

"You'll never sell any copies of your book if you take that attitude," said my wife Norman, again getting the wrong end of the stick.

Friday

The Telegraph rang me this morning, even before I had poured out my plate of Waitrose Own-Brand "Choc-o-Krispies" (which, to my mind, are markedly inferior to the original Kellogg's Coco-Pops).

"It's about the book," they said. "At last," I replied, "a serious newspaper is taking my book seriously." "Oh no," they said, "it's not your book we're interested in. It's the one by Mrs Chaplin, your former secretary. We wondered if you had any comment on her claim that you were totally obsessed by Mrs Thatcher and used to storm round Number 10 shouting 'Exterminate, exterminate' like a dalek whenever her name was mentioned."

"That is an outrageous lie," I said. "I expect Mrs Thatcher is behind this. In my judgement that woman should be exterminated."

Saturday

Today was the highlight of my promotional tour. Mr Fishwick had arranged a special "Signing Session" in the Raynes Park branch of Books R Us. In the window there was a photo of me in my cricket clothes, with a sign in big letters saying "Local Author" because I used to live there. There was also a large pile of three of my books waiting for the queues to form when I began the signing session.

I was there for no small measure of time, ie two hours, and no one came in at all, which was not inconsiderably disappointing. "Never mind," said the kindly assistant, a young man with an earring in his nose. "No one buys books by politicians. Unless of course you are Mrs Thatcher," he laughed.

Just then my first customer arrived, in the shape of my brother Terry. "I thought I might catch you here, John," he said. "I read your book and I just wanted to tell you that it is full of mistakes. For instance, on page 712 you referred to our pet squirrel as Cyril, whereas he was actually called Len after the famous cricketer Sir Leonard Hutton."

He went on in this tiresome and outrageous fashion for a very not inconsiderable amount of time. I could only wish that my brother was "long-lost" like Mrs Lemon. Oh yes.

© Fishcock and Tweed

THE SUNDAY TIMES

12 NOVEMBER 1999

Queen Humiliated By Australian Poll

by Our Political Staff Rupert Murdoch

THE British Monarchy was dealt a devastating blow today when millions of ordinary Australians voted to retain the Queen as the country's constitutional Head of State.

Palace insiders admitted that the Queen had been "devastated", "wounded" and "bloody gutted, mate" when the news was broken to her that only the majority of the country wanted her to stay on as Queen.

Sources close to Her Majesty confirmed to the Sunday Times that the Queen had been "close

RESULTS IN FULL	
Boomerang North	
Yeah mate:	56%
No mate:	24%
Don't give a XXXX:	26%
Castlemaine South	
(That's enough results. Ed.)	

to suicide", but only the thought of Prince Charles becoming King had persuaded her not to take this drastic step.

Britain Next

Leading Republicans, on the other hand, were jubilant. Parties

went on all night and old-age pensioners danced in the streets with their young Oriental wives.

William Shakespeare and Sir Walter Raleigh go into business

What You Will Read

An exclusive extract from the sizzling roman-à-clef by William Hague's right-hand PR woman. It's the book that everyone in London is talking about but not buying!

SCANTIES
by Amanda Platell

Chapter One

MIRANDA BLATELL was the gorgeous editor of the *Sexpress on Sunday*, the best-selling, highest circulation newspaper with all the best stories that *(Get on with juicy bits. Ed.)*

Miranda walked into the office of glamorous, young, sexy, Tory leader, William Vague.

"You said you wanted me," she giggled naughtily, slipping off her coat to reveal her perfectly formed body wearing nothing but La Bollarda silk underwear.

"How can I help you, Mr Vague?" she breathed huskily with the Australian lilt that had bewitched every editor in Fleet Street – except the female ones who were all fat, stupid cows who weren't beautiful like she was. It was pathetic really the way these frumpy old dykes were so consumed with jealousy for anyone who showed the slightest talent, especially if they were good looking as well. And now she had written a brilliant book and had her picture in all the papers *(Get on with the bit where you and Hague have it away on the desk. Ed.)*

"I'm very worried about our stance on the Euro," the baseball-hatted Tory superstud growled.

"Take me! Take me!" I screamed in ecstasy.

The End

ST PAUL TO APPEAR ON PARKY SHOW

by Our Chat Show Staff CLIVE JAMES ANDERSON

THE WORLD'S greatest-ever chat show host Michael Parkinson has pulled off an astonishing coup by persuading St Paul of McTarsus to make his first television appearance since he died 2000 years ago.

WHAT YOU WILL SEE

Parky *(for it is he)*: It is my very great privilege to welcome tonight one of the greatest figures of the last two millennia. A big hand for St Paul!

(Hysterical applause as barefoot

man enters eating veggieburger)

Parky *(consults notes)*: How did it all begin, all those thousands of years ago?

St Paul: Well, there was four of us in them days – St John, St George and the other one who does the Thomas the Tank Engine voiceover. But that's not important, Michael. What I want to talk about is what happened to me on this great tour we did of Damascus.

Parky *(reading autocue)*: And what did happen?

St Paul: I saw the light and that,

Michael. I was on the road, and I was eating this lamb kebab which one of the roadies had got for me. And then this light came through the window, and I heard this voice calling out "Paul, Paul, why are you eating me?" And it was this sheep. But it wasn't really a sheep. It was more like Linda, sort of dressed up as a sheep. Anyway, from that moment I've eaten nothing but veggieburgers.

Parky: Incredible. That's the most incredible story I've ever heard! Can you tell us some more about that?

St Paul: It is incredible, Michael, but even more incredible is my new album which is dedicated to the vegetableburger-eating community all over the world. And all the other worlds that we live in simultaneously. I mean, have you ever thought, Michael, that we could at this very moment be appearing on millions of other chat shows in billions of other galaxies?

Parky: That's absolutely incredible! Fantastic! Would you like to mime to one of the tracks?

St Paul: I'd love to, Michael, that's why I agreed to come on.

(Group plays 'Band's Got The Runs [They've Eaten Too Many Veggieburgers]')

A video of this historic interview is now available for only £25.99 from BBC Enterprises.

That Aussie Republican Referendum...

THE QUEEN IS A - BONZER SHEILA / POMMIE BASTARD

SPUD AS U LIKE IT

DAILY MAIL

French Feed British Tourists To Cattle

by Our Diplomatic Staff MADDIE TUPP

IN AN extraordinary new development in the so-called Beef War, the Mail has learned that most French cattle are actually fed the remains of British holiday-makers who have mysteriously disappeared whilst taking a short continental break.

Said one witness who did not wish to be named (because he is the editor of the Daily Mail), "This is just the sort of thing you would expect the French to do. I would imagine that one minute the English family were sitting in a café having an agreeable glass of vin rouge and the next they were travelling down the second stomach of a French cow."

The Mail Says:

Don't Buy The Following French Goods!

- French onions
- French lettuce
- French letters
- French and Saunders.

THE SUN SAYS

THE French are disgusting. How dare they feed sewage to defenceless dumb animals who have no idea what they are consuming. That is the *Sun*'s job and one which we do with pride.

On Other Pages

Rod and Caprice, Michael and Zeta, Tit and Bum, PLUS Garry Bushell.

Remember

There's more sewage in the Sun!

YOUR DINNER IS IN THE TOILET

THAT FRENCH TRADE WAR IN FULL

FRENCH BOYCOTT	NICK BROWN BOYCOTT
200,000 Tonnes of British Beef	2 Bottles of that nice Beaujolais they sell in Sainsbury's
	One pain au chocolat from that lovely little patisserie near Jeremy's house
	One baguette I was going to get for Sebastian's picnic...
	Oh yes, and the Camembert that Phillip likes as well.
Value: £4,000,000	**Value: £6.24**

HAVE YOU SEEN THIS MAN?

Police would very much like to know the whereabouts of this man in relation to a series of deceptions carried out recently in the Bournemouth area which resulted in the disappearance of a large number of bobbies on the beat.

They warn that if he remains at large he could threaten the public's safety. If you see him, inform a policeman immediately – if you can find one.

If you can't find a policeman, then just shout "Free Tibet!" loudly and three hundred will immediately appear and beat you up.

★ Exclusive to all lazy newspapers ★

WAS WOODHOUSE A NAZI?

by Our Illiterary Staff Gussie Fink-Little

ONE OF the country's best-loved literary figures was yesterday revealed to be a Nazi sympathiser by a set of documents released under the Thirty-Year-Old Story Rule.

The papers appear to show that Barbara Woodhouse, author of *Fetch!* and *Heel Boy!* was in the pay of the German High Command for the latter part of the First World War. (*Subs – please check.*)

The circumstantial evidence against Woodhouse is overwhelming, say experts I haven't had time to talk to, who point out the following sinister facts:

1. She insisted on her orders being obeyed.

2. She liked wearing a "uniform" of tweed skirt and sensible shoes.

3. She went walkies into the Sudetenland. (*No, she didn't. This is rubbish. Ed.*)

All in all, the picture now emerging of P.G. Woodhouse, known as "Tips" to her colleagues, is of a committed dog-handler who would stop at nothing to bring about the Thousand-Year Reich. (*You're fired. Ed.*)

PROOF FROM THE ARCHIVES

Sieg Heil, Jeeves!

Very good, Sir

THE SCENE THAT I WILL NEVER FORGET

by Phil Ghoul

IN THE early morning mist they stood there in the deserted car park. Four solitary cars. Abandoned. Alone, where they had been standing all night.

Mute witnesses to the tragedy that they did not know would happen when they parked here.

Ghostly sentinels of doom.

A thin layer of frost coating my laptop as I tried to imagine how people would feel when they had to read this stuff.

In the silence, there was the strangled sound of a mobile phone. It was my editor asking me to go back to Paddington and write another thousand words about the twisted mass of metal bearing tragic witness to *(continued in all papers)*

> Counsellors are available for readers of the above piece who may be in a state of shock.

GOOD THINKING JOHN — WE'VE PRIVATISED THE BLAME

GOVERNMENT PLEDGES TO SHUT STABLE DOOR — 'WHATEVER THE COST'

by Our Rail Transport Staff

JOHN PRESCOTT today gave a firm undertaking to spend as much money as was necessary to close the stable door after the recent "bolting" incident.

"The stable door must be shut," he told reporters. "And I have launched an immediate initiative to get it closed as soon as possible."

He continued, "This government is absolutely committed to ensuring that the stable door incident is never repeated, even if it costs as much money as they told us it would five years ago before the horse bolted."

On Other Pages

■ Shocking number of pounds tragically lost as safety devices implemented **7**

PRESCOTT ANNOUNCES NEW SAFETY PROCEDURES

by Our Rail Correspondent
Paddington Blair

THE Transport Secretary, Mr John Prescott, yesterday unveiled sweeping new measures to ensure that safety is the number one priority for those involved in public transport.

Speaking from the mobile phone in his car, he told newsmen that he had a comprehensive 10-point plan for what action to take to prevent disaster.

THAT PLAN IN FULL

1. Blame Railtrack.
2. Blame the operating companies.
3. Announce a 10-point plan.
4. Go to work in your chauffeur-driven car.
5. Er...
6. That's it.

"Once you have completed this operation," said Mr Prescott, "your job as transport minister will be absolutely safe."

PADDINGTON STATION

INQUIRIES   PUBLIC INQUIRIES

LATE NEWS

NEW RAILTRACK DISASTER

THERE was mounting concern last night for the safety of Richard Middleton, the commercial director of Railtrack, who failed to spot the danger signals and crashed straight into the *Today* programme.

"We couldn't stop him," said horrified onlooker John Humphrys. "He just ploughed on, calling the public hysterical and claiming that rail travel was safe the day after another accident."

A Railtrack spokesman immediately denied that Richard Middleton was dangerous and anyone who said otherwise was just "hysterical".

YES! IT'S OFFICIAL TORY MAYORAL CANDIDATE RHYMING SLANG!

Tea Leaf = Controversial past

IN THE COURTS

Fayed v. Regina
Day 94

Before Mr Justice Cocklecarrot

An appeal against the refusal of the Home Secretary to grant a passport to a distinguished foreign businessman.

Michael Ballsoff Q.C.: M'Lud, I am appearing for the money.

Cocklecarrot: Surely, Mr Ballsache, that cannot be right.

Ballsoff: I am indebted to you, M'Lud. I am appearing for the plaintiff.

Fayed: Get it fuggin' right, you stupid fugger. That's what I pay you for.

Cocklecarrot: Please continue, Mr Ballsup.

Ballsup: M'Lud, you see before you a man of sorrows and acquainted with grief. I am referring to my unhappy client, Mr Fugger.

Fayed: It's Al-Fugger, you stupid fugger.

Ballsup: My Lord, my client is a man who has been most grievously wronged. At a time when he was still in mourning for the tragic death of his son…

Cocklecarrot: Is this in any way relevant to the issue of the passport, Mr Ballsup?

Ballsup: Of course not, M'Lud.

Cocklecarrot: Just checking!

(Laughter)

Ballsup: My Lord, if you are good enough to turn to Bundle B, you will find that my client has made regular payments to Conservative MPs.

Cocklecarrot: Can that be right, Mr Bollockoff?

Ballsitup: I mean, of course, regular payments to the Inland Revenue, M'Lud. I am indebted to you.

Cocklecarrot: As indeed are the Tory MPs!

(More laughter)

Fayed: I told you it wouldn't fuggin' work. Give him the fuggin' money.

(Usher hands brown envelope to judge)

Ballsoff: Can I refer to the bundle of notes which Your Lordship might like to consider in the privacy of his own safe?

Cocklecarrot: I think I've heard enough of this rubbish. Nut-case dismissed! Geddit?!

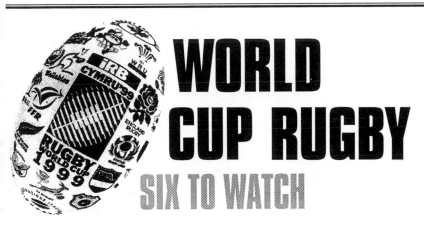

WORLD CUP RUGBY
SIX TO WATCH

Diertie Baastaad, legendary No. 17 of the South African All Whites. At 22 stone, Baastaad is bound to leave his mark on the opposition's face.

Puncho Gauja, legendary Argentinian hooker who, at 44 stone, has caught the eye of a lot of his opponents with his fingers.

Hujabugga Bollabreaka, legendary 33-stone Samoan full back famed for his kicking ability. Once converted the opposing scrum half from his own 20-yard line.

Jonah Whale, legendary 59-ton New Zealand giant mammal famed for his ability to swallow the entire England team whole.

Kanga Roo, legendary 7ft 9ins Australian line-out specialist, willing to take the fight to the other side, usually with his trademark boxing gloves.

Garry Du Lally, legendary English 24 milligram cocaine expert famous for denying ever scoring anything *(That's enough Rugby. Ed.)*

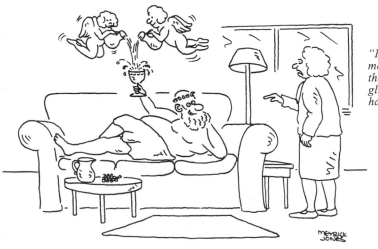

"It's become more than just the occasional glass of wine, hasn't it?"

MARCH OF THE APPRENTICE PAPERBOY

The feature is orange!

TV Highlights

Channel Four
The Bore War: 1999-2001

With the aid of contemporary archive footage, this award-winning documentary series reconstructs the desperate fight of the Bores to avoid extinction against the overwhelming forces of the Blairish Empire. Clinging to their archaic beliefs and way of life under their uncharismatic leader Willem Van Der Hague, they fought a series of rearguard actions, as the Blairish occupied all their traditional ground. Highlights include the Relief of Ladythatch, the Fall of Majorking and the Battle of Not Much Kop, where the Bores were finally wiped out. **Narrated by TV's Charles Bore.**

POETRY CORNER

**In Memoriam
Inspector Morse**

So. Farewell
Then
Inspector Morse.

The opera-loving
TV detective.

You have now
Gone to a
Better place
For eternity.

U.K. Gold.

> Endeavour J. Thribb (17½ pints)

In Memoriam L!ve TV

So. Farewell
Then
L!ve TV.

Brainchild of Kelvin
Mackenzie and
Janet Street-Porter.

Home of Topless
Darts, The Weather
In Norwegian
And News
Bunny.

Now
Ironically
You are
Dead.

> E.J. Thribb (17½ viewers)

**In Memoriam Sir Larrold
"Larry" Lamb, Editor of
the Sun newspaper**

So. Farewell then
Sir Larry Lamb,
Inventor of the famous
"Page Three Girl".

"Gorgeous, pouting
Samantha, 19,
Is certainly keen to show off
Her talents."
That was your catchphrase.

"Phew! What a scorcher!"
That was another,
Which you might be
Using again —
Depending on where you
Have gone.

> E.J. Thribb (17½)

IT'S GRIM UP NORTH LONDON — KNIFE & PACKER

IT'S GRIM UP NORTH LONDON KNIFE & PACKER

In Memoriam Desmond Llewellyn, Actor

So. Farewell then
"Q"
Armourer to James Bond
In all
94 films.

Inventor of the tootbrush
That turned into
A speedboat.
And the cufflink that became
An atomic bomb.

"Now listen carefully
Double-0 7."
That was your catchphrase.

"Don't touch that, Bond!"
That was another.

It will not be the same
With John Cleese.

Keith says
"Dead parrots will not help you
Escape from SMERSH."
(No disrespect intended to
Our foremost "Python!")

E.J. Thribb (17½)

In Memoriam Ernest Lough, Famous Boy Soprano

So. Farewell then
Ernest Lough,
Famous boy soprano.

"O For The Wings
Of A Dove."

That was your catchphrase.

And now
You've probably got them.

Ernest J. Thribb
Boy Poet (aged 13½)

In Memoriam Mr Takeshita, former Prime Minister of Japan

So. Farewell then
Mr Takeshita,
Japanese politician
And the world's
Most famous
Anagram.

So. Farewell then also
To this joke
Which dies
With you.

E.J. Thribb (17½)

MAD KOW-TOW DISEASE HITS BRITAIN

**by Our Medical Staff
Dr James Le Fumanchu**

A SERIOUS outbreak of the disease OBN, known colloquially as "Mad Kow-Tow Disease", swept Britain yesterday as hundreds of victims fell to their knees and dribbled in front of visiting Chinese dignitaries.

The disease, which affects the brain, leaves the sufferer with no critical faculties at all and results in severe memory loss – some of the worst cases end up forgetting everything they ever knew about the Chinese record on human rights.

CHAIRMAN MOO

Doctors believe that Mad Kow-Tow disease is caused by eating too much humble pie which attacks the nervous system, thus making the host extremely anxious about losing trade contracts.

At this point, the backbone begins to crumble, eventually disintegrating completely, leaving its pathetic former owner a grinning mass of jelly who can only gibber "Welcome to Britain, Your Excellency".

That Chinese Royal Official Banquet Menu In Full

Brown Tongue Windsor Soup
Grovelax on Brown-Nose Bread and Butter Up
✳
Supreme Chicken Out or Peking Duck-Issues
Toady-In-The-Hole With Appease Pudding
✳
Tiananmusu (off)
Cowardy Custard
✳
Petit Gang of Fours

All served on Willow No-Patten China

To drink: Chateau Sycofantin-Latour '61 and a selection of Arsliqueurs

The Banquet Music In Full
Played By The Band of the 14/21st Queen's Own Buskers

At the entrance
Pimp and Circumstance . . . . Elgar

Over dinner
Medley: Songs from the shows
A Nightingale was Shot in Tiananmen Square – Tanks for the Memory – Kiss Me Kate Adie

After the speeches
Drool Britannia . . . . Parry
God Save Zemin . . . . Trad.

World Exclusive
Chinese Leader Granted Audience

One of the most historic interviews in the history of the world took place last week on the eve of the State visit to London by His Imperial Magnificence Comrade Jiang Zemin.

The interview was conducted by His Grace the Lord Mogg, Ambassador Plenipotentiary from the Court of St Rupert. Their conversation took place in the Hall of A Thousand Suns, in the Palace of Heavenly Boredom, just off Tiananmen Square.

Lord Rice-Mogg: Your Holiness, it is extremely good of you to spare a few minutes in the middle of your extraordinarily busy life as the ruler over 8 billion people to talk to a humble antiquarian bookseller from Somerset...

Zemin: Get on with it.

Mogg: ...ha, ha, ha. I am privileged to witness an example of your legendary wit at first hand.

Zemin: Ask me about the trade figures.

Mogg: May I now ask you about the trade figures?

Zemin: I am glad you asked me about that. In the past five years alone the gross domestic product of the People's Republic of China has risen by no less than 1.36 million percent.

Mogg: Is that because of your brilliant leadership?

Zemin: Indeed it is *(smiles benignly)*. Ask me about the modernisation of China.

Mogg: May I turn now to a somewhat controversial subject: the modernisation of your great country of which you are the revered helmsman.

Zemin: China is modernising at an astonishing rate. Everywhere you look you will see skyscrapers, mobile telephones and lap-top computers.

Mogg: And I couldn't help noticing also on my way here a large number of Mr Murdoch's Sky Satellite televisual devices.

Zemin: That was what you call a commercial break?

Mogg: Very, very amusing, your Highness. Ha, ha, ha. And now that we are getting on so well, perhaps this would be an opportune moment to raise the delicate issue of the different ways in which different countries choose to sort out their own internal problems, each doubtless valid in their own way.

Zemin: Ah, you mean Tibet. Normally, I shoot people at this point of the interview! But since you have raised this question in such a tactful way, while lying flat out on the floor and applying your tongue to my shoe, I will spare your miserable life.

Mogg: You are too generous, Your Supreme Majesty.

Zemin: Your time is up.

Mogg: Perhaps before I pay the supreme penalty for my impertinence, I might be allowed to present you with this Moroccan bound copy of yesterday's *Sun* newspaper bearing the headline "IT'S RICE TO SEE YOU JIANG! YOU'RE OUR NUMBER WON-SUN!".

Zemin: Guards, take him away.

© *Moggtrash Productions, in association with Times Newspapers Plc.*

*"As far as I'm aware, Mrs Grey, there **is** no cure for happiness"*

From the best-selling author of Born To Be Queen, Heir of Sorrows *and* La Dame Aux Camillas, *now comes the greatest love story of them all.*

Never Too Old...

by Dame Sylvie Krin

THE STORY SO FAR: Multi-media tycoon Rupert Murdoch and his lovely young bride Wendy are playing host to the President of China at an exhibition of priceless Oriental antiquities.

Now read on...

THE FABLED Great Hall of the British Museum had never seen anything like it. On every side the glass cases were piled high with the exquisite masterpieces of the world's oldest civilisation.

Here at the entrance stood the Golden Dragon of Feng Shui, with its emerald eyes, which had once stood guard at the Summer Palace of the Dung Emperors.

There, facing it, a life-size terracotta warrior, from the 8th Century tomb of the Dowager Widow Twan-ki.

"I hope this pile of junk impresses our friend Fu Manchu," whispered the global entrepreneur into the delicate porcelain ear of his young wife, "'cos it certainly bores the shit out of me."

"Be quiet, Rupert, your guests are here."

As she spoke, a fanfare of trumpets heralded the arrival of President Zemin, followed at a respectful four paces by the Queen of England with her husband and a huge crowd of dignitaries.

"What the hell's she doing here?" the ageing republican hissed angrily. "I didn't give her an invite."

"Shut up, Rupert, she's the head of state."

"Not for long, if my newspapers have anything to do with it."

He was interrupted by an equerry tapping him on the shoulder. "Your Majesty, may I introduce Mr Murdoch, who has very kindly sponsored this exhibition?"

"Murdoch?" smiled the Queen, extending a gloved hand. "I hope you're nothing to do with that ghastly Australian man who owns the dirty little newspapers that my late daughter-in-law used to be so keen on?"

"At your service, ma'am," breathed the proprietor of the Sun and the News of the World. "It's a fair cop."

Before their polite badinage could develop further, the imposing figure of the Chinese head of state and First Secretary of the Communist Party loomed over them, his face contorted with rage.

"Imperialist lobbers," he shouted at the bewildered monarch, waving an arm at the exhibits. "Evelything rooted flom Chinese people."

"That's enough from you, slitty-eyes," interposed the Queen's consort, "any more of this nonsense and we'll take back Hong Kong."

A delicate frown creased the cherry blossom visage of the nubile young goddess from the land of egg-fried rice.

This was not how their great evening was meant to go at all. It was terrible...

"IT WAS terrible," said Sir Gavin Sewell, the neatly-bearded Curator of the Museum's Oriental Department, as the party stood in front of a priceless silk screen dating back to the early years of the Ping Pong Dynasty.

"Here, Your Excellency – and not forgetting Your Majesty, we can see the ancient story of the elderly merchant who made the foolish mistake of marrying a beautiful young bride, whom he had found working in one of his rice fields."

With an elegantly manicured finger he pointed to the middle panel of the screen.

"The old man was so besotted by her that he did everything she asked. Little did he know that he would be so exhausted by her constant amorous demands that he would end up dying a premature death, leaving her the richest woman in China."

A ripple of appreciative laughter ran round his distinguished audience.

"What a plonker falling for that one," commented the Duke of Edinburg rather too loudly, "must be all that rice they eat."

There was one member of the party, however, who for some reason had not found the old Chinese legend so amusing.

As the Royal party moved off, Rupert remained staring thoughtfully at the picture of the old merchant on his death bed, as his young wife counted out piles of gold in the background.

What was it that disturbed him, marring what was to have been his special day...?

To be continued

QUEEN HONOURS CHARLES

...and what do you do?

"It's very nice of your husband to sit for our little group, Sandra"

OLDEST PEER LEAVES FOR THE LAST TIME

by Our Constitutional Reform Staff **Ex-Lord Snooty**

IT WAS a sad day at the Palace of Westminster when Britain's oldest peer, Lord Dino of Saur, returned to his country seat at Jurassic Park (8 million acres).

Said the departing peer, "My family has served this country for over twenty million years. My ancestors roamed freely here long before Tony Blair and his like had even evolved."

He continued, "We have not had one word of thanks for all we have done to keep this country free from diplodoci."

He concluded, "It would have been courteous for Baroness Jay to have come round for supper to be eaten by myself and Lady Dina Saur."

Lord Dino of Saur is the 147 millionth Baron Swamp.

BLAIR GETS TOUGH ON DOWN AND OUTS

by Our Social Affairs Staff **Peers Morgan**

THE GOVERNMENT launched an offensive yesterday to rid the country of the spectacle of people "sleeping rough" on benches in the House of Lords.

Said Hopeless Czar, Margaret Jay, "You can't encourage these people by giving them a nice lunch and a warm place to sleep."

"You've got to get tough and kick them off the benches without a penny," she continued.

SOUP OF THE JAY

"This will force them to find something better to do than lie around getting in the way of the government."

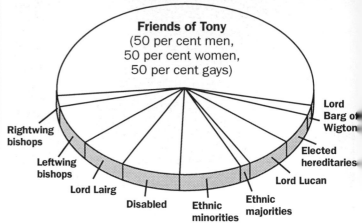
 by T H E 4 t h E A R L O F H U S B A N D

AMAZING LEGAL BREAKTHROUGH

Two Men Will Father New Baby For First Time

by Our Science Staff **M. Brio**

HISTORY was made today when, for the first time, two men were both named as leaders of a newly-reborn political party.

The two men, named as Michael and William, have enjoyed "a stable relationship" for more than ten minutes.

They told waiting newsmen that they were "over the moon" at being allowed to play the joint role of father to the tiny party.

The surrogate mother is believed to be an elderly London woman, a "Mrs T.", who said she was "very happy" for the two young men.

"They are both very caring people," she said, "and I am very pleased to hand over to them the party to which I gave birth in the 1980s."

ON OTHER PAGES

Can the baby survive?
by Dr Thomas Utterfraud **7**

The Enterprise Culture

Chris Evans

Wedding Of The Century

Geri Halliwell

How They Are Related

Dame Edith Evans	Vincent Halliwell
Dame Harold Evans	Ginger Rodgers
Sir Christopher Bland	Rodgers & Halliwell
Christopher Robin	Rodgers & Hammerstein
Robin 'Ginger' Cook	Geri and the Spicemakers
Richard 'Ginger' Branson	Geri Hallomagazine
Christopher Biggins	**Jerry Hall**

VILLAGE PEOPLE TO REFORM

GINGER IN LOVE WITH GINGER

by Our Celebrity Staff **Phil Spice**

CHRIS EVANS has told friends that he has fallen deeply and hopelessly in love with the ginger-haired star of TFI Friday.

Their whirlwind romance began when Evans spotted himself in the mirror across a crowded room.

"It was love at first sight," said Chris. "I was instantly attracted to Ginger. He's so talented and good-looking," he continued, "not to mention modest."

The relationship blossomed when Evans appeared with himself on his hit Channel 4 show "Thank God It's Nearly Over".

There was an instant and visible rapport with Chris flirting outrageously with himself for the whole programme.

Evans has admitted to colleagues that he wants to spend the rest of his life with the brilliant Virgin Radio boss.

"This time it's for good," he said. "No one could love me more than I do."
© *Matthew Fraud PR*

That Queen's Speech In Full

"My Government has done a wonderful job of making Britain a much happier, more successful country. Everywhere one goes, one sees happy, smiling, healthy, well-educated people saying 'Isn't it wonderful what my Government has done?'

"My Government is not stopping there. My Government will introduce a number of measures to make things even more wonderful.

"My Government therefore urges everyone to vote Labour in gratitude, or should I say 'to gratefully vote Labour' which is the correct usage in the New Queen's English, where we are all entitled to happily split infinitives.

"A Happy Christmas to you all."

© *Her Majesty the Prime Minister.*

LABOUR NOUVEAU IS 'BIG FLOP'

by Our Political Staff **Phil Glass**

ONCE the cry of "Le Labour Nouveau est arrivé!" would have the middle-classes cheering and rushing to their nearest polling station.

But no more. This year's vintage has been branded "over-hyped, thin stuff which leaves a nasty taste in the mouth".

Experts say that the current batch "barely qualifies as red".

BLAIRJOLAIS

At tastings round the country consumers registered their disappointment.

"We thought Labour Nouveau would be an exciting new experience," said one, "but actually it's lightweight, unpleasant and increasingly hard to swallow."

LORD ARCHER RHYMING SLANG

Berkeley Hunt = Me

"Do you wanna be in my gang..."

GARY GROCER GUILTY

by Our Filth Staff
Blue Max Clifford Chatterley

THE AGEING former prime minister Gary Grocer (real name Edward Heath) yesterday denied sensational allegations in a downmarket Sunday newspaper (the Sunday Telegraph) that he had "an unhealthy secret passion" for dictators.

The newspaper had claimed that Heath was "in love" with a long succession of power-crazed over-age tyrants, ranging from the late Mao Tse-Tung to the late Marshal Tito.

GROCER INDECENCY

Looking raddled and paunchy, the disgraced former prime minister defended himself, claiming that the press had attempted to smear him by digging up true stories about his past.

"I have nothing to be ashamed of," he said. "It is quite true that I met these people on a number of occasions, and we may have exchanged gifts, but it went no further than that.

"To accuse me of tyrantophilia is plainly ludicrous. Chairman Mao was a very nice man, unlike Dominic Lawson, who is a rude, bad-tempered bully just like myself."

Grocer Heath is 97.

Secret loves of the Grocer — pics pp. 18-26

GLITTER VICTIM SPEAKS OUT

by Our Reporter **Pippa Ratzi**

THE TRAGIC woman at the centre of the Gary Glitter case previously only known as Miss X has come forward, so as to let the world know the horror she's experienced.

"I was just a naïve innocent girl," she said in a trembling voice, "when a filthy old man came to my door and offered me £10,000 if I'd do things for him, things that I knew were wrong. But Max was very persuasive and wouldn't take no for an answer. The next thing I knew he was thrusting a huge cheque at me from the News of the World he worked for, and I became putty in his hands.

"How can these sick perverts be allowed to prey on innocent girls like me? Of course, he promised he'd look after me but as soon as he got what he wanted and the story was published he was off like a shot."

Since Gary Glitter was cleared of the charges, Alison says the memory of losing her £25,000 bonus will haunt her for many years to come.

■ **More sanctimonious self-serving guff pp. 2-98**

BLAIR BABY SHOCK!

I don't know how it leaked out

You Name The People's Baby

Boys	Girls
Tony	Tonyella
Peter	Posh Spice
Alastair	Diana
Not Gordon	Not Harriet
Rupert	Maggie
Lord Bragg of Wigton	Baroness Jay

Phone now on the BLAIR BABE HOTLINE and win a pair of free tickets to hit musical *Tess of the D'Urbervilles*.

Spot The Baby

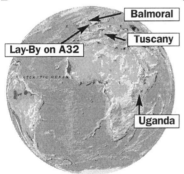

The Daily Telegraph invites you to put a cross where you think the Blair bun went into the oven!

● **Phone now on the Spot The Baby Hotline and win two pairs of tickets to hit musical** *Tess of the D'Urbervilles.*

Apology

IN the last few days we, in common with all other newspapers, may have given the impression that we thought Cherie Blair was looking in some way dowdy and frumpy.

Headlines such as **"Is this the world's worst dressed woman?"**, **"The Frocky Horror Show"** and **"Nightmare on Dowdy Street"** may have reinforced this inference.

We now realise that there was not a jot or scintilla of truth in any of the above and that Cherie Blair is in fact an extraordinarily beautiful woman blooming with health and happiness and radiating an inner joy that transcends mere fashion.

We would like to apologise unreservedly to Mrs Blair for any distress that our earlier reports may inadvertently have caused.

GLENDA SLAGG

The Mother of All Fleet Street!

ROYAL BABY SPECIAL

HATS OFF to Cherie Blair! Didn't you shed a little tear when you heard the nooz that Mr Stork would be poppin' down the chimney at Number Ten with a little bundle of joy!?!?!

What wonderful tidings for all us gals of a certain age who thought that the pitter patter of tiny feet would never be heard again??!? All together now – Aaah!!!!

CHERIE BLAIR – what a thoughtless cow??!?! Doesn't she know how dangerous it is to have a kiddie at her age!?!? What a selfish thing to do??! By the time the little toddler is ten, Tony will have one foot in the grave and she'll be waiting in for Meals on Wheels!?? What sort of life is that for a littl'un to look forward to?? No football in the park for him or her – just pushing the old folks round in their wheelchairs??! All together now – Uuuurgh!!?

THREE CHEERS for Cherie and Tony!?!? At last there's someone who believes in the family!?! The stuffy corridors of Number Ten will for the first time resound to the sound of a happy infant a-crawlin' and a-bawlin', a-cooin' and a-poo-in'!! All together now – coochee coochee coo!!!?!

TONY BLAIR – what was he thinking of?!? Who wants the Prime Minister kept awake at night when he should be thinking about Northern Ireland!!?! We want his mind on the job – and not that one, mister!!? All together now – Boochee! Boochee! Boo!

HATS AND trousers off to Blair!? Here's one world leader who has got lead in his pencil?!! And isn't it heartwarming that at Tony and Cherie's age the candle of love is still burning bright??! Pass me the tissues, Mister Reader, I've just gotta have a li'l weep!!

WILLIAM HAGUE and Ffion take note!! You two should be having a good Fff-un time between the sheets!?! (Geddit??) Or you'll be washed up Fffor ever!?! Geddit???!

HERE THEY ARE – Glenda's Debonair Dads!?!

TONY BLAIR: He's put Cherie into New Labour!?! Geddit???

THE PRIME MINISTER: He can have his Third Way with me any time!?!?

TONY: Why stop at four children – let's go for Number Ten!! (Geddit??!?) Keep it up, Tone!! (Geddit?!?!) Time for a big election!! *(That's enough filth. Ed.)*

Byebee!!!! Geddit!?!?!

23

Daily Mail

FRIDAY, NOVEMBER 12, 1999   NATIONAL NEWSPAPER OF THE YEAR 35p

Beef War Latest

I SEE OUR GALLANT COWS GO IN

By LUNCHTIME O'MOOS

TODAY I saw with my own eyes thousands of British cows storm ashore in France, to recapture the continent for British beef.

After years of waiting, the feeling of excitement was tangible.

At last, our plucky cows were going to show the sewage-eating, garlic-swilling Frogs and Krauts what they were made of (95 percent water, 4 percent growth-promoting hormones, 1 percent BSE).

CJD-Day

As they stormed up the beaches, they were met by a solid wall of highly-trained French and German officials, determined to hurl them back into the sea.

It was a disaster. Wave upon wave of cows, stranded on the beach, hoping against hope for a miracle.

And then, as if a prayer were answered, out of the mist emerged the flotilla of little shits *(Surely 'boats'? Ed.)* led by skipper Nick Brown.

Dunkow

Within seconds, the heroic cows were sailing back to Blighty and the safety of a good old British abattoir.

It was our finest hour.

The Moron Says

Jail This Man

HE HAS made up stories. He has lied. He has misled millions of people. Put me in jail at once.

© P. Moron, Editor, The Daily Moron.

OLD QUEEN DEAD

A Nation Mourns

THE much-loved figure of Her Royal Highness the Quentin of Crisp has passed away in her 90th year.

With her trademark flowery hats, handbag and purple hair, she charmed the nation through nine decades of dedicated public life.

She was the darling of the armed forces and was loved by soldiers, airmen and particularly sailors.

Said one elderly guardsman, "I was deeply touched in St James's Park. It was a meeting I shall never forget."

Said Royal watcher Sir Neddington Twinkswell, 72, "She is irreplaceable. The younger generation do not have the style or the grace to carry it off. The young queens of today are not in the same league."

Souvenir packet of Quentin flavoured crisps available from Gnome Offers, Unit 94, The Trading Estate, Welwyn Garden City.

MARCH OF THE APPRENTICE PAPERBOY II

It's a front-page sash!

PROTEST AT 'DISGRACEFUL PORTRAYAL OF JESUS'

by Our Religious Affairs Staff **Phil Pews**

HUGE numbers of gay protestors have been picketing churches over their weekly depiction of Christ as "the son of God who redeemed mankind".

Said spokesman St Peter of Tatchell: "I am sick of seeing one of the world's most revered homosexuals characterised as a preacher, healer and spiritual leader.

"There is no evidence to support this view of Christ. The only historical facts that are known for sure are that Christ was a militant Palestinian gay rights activist who was arrested and martyred for his homosexual beliefs."

He continued: "This perverted version of the truth must be stopped and I am calling for the closure of all these churches, who are only putting on controversial material as a cheap publicity stunt to get themselves an audience."

ARCHER SHOCK

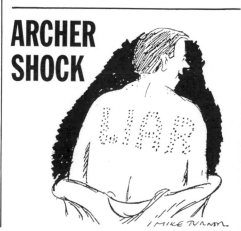

24

That Honorary Degree Citation In Full

SALUTAMUS CHERRYBRANDYENSIS BLAIRISSIMA (NATA BOOTHA) FILIA ANTONIUS BOOZUS (THESPIANUS NOTORIUS IN VIA CORONATIONE ET SCOUSUS GITTUS IN COMEDIA SERIALIS USQUE AD MORTEM CUM ALFREDO GARNETTO); UXOR PULCHERRIMA AD ANTONIO BLAIRISSIMO, CAESAR MAGNIFICUS ET OMNIPOTENTIS, SUPREMUS DUX UNIVERSALIS, PONTIFEX MAXIMUS ET REVERENDUS SANCTUS ALBIONENSIS. SED IN TUA PROPRIA PERSONA, ADVOCATA SUPERBA ET OPULENTA, PUPILLA FAVORITA DERRIUS IRVINI (DOMINE LAIRGI). SED SUPRA OMNIA, MATER FECUNDISSIMA AD XLV ANNOS, CONCEPTIONIS MIRACULOSUS ET CONVENIENTUS. STUPOR MUNDI! GAUDEAMUS! GLORIA IN EXCELSIS BLAIRO!

© UNIVERSITATE WESTMONASTERIUM (QUONDAM POLYTECHNICO BARBICANO NEASDENSIS QUIK-SAVE SPONSORIS) MCMIX.

HUGE PILE OF MONEY OPENED IN COVENT GARDEN

By Our Opera Staff **Don G. O'Money**

A GLITTERING array of celebrities, headed by Her Majesty the Queen and the Prime Minister Tony Blair, last night attended the gala opening of the Royal Pile of Money in London's fashionable Covent Garden.

It had taken almost a quarter of a century to amass the most splendid collection of money London has ever seen.

There were gasps of amazement as the curtains parted to reveal a vast mountain of £50 pound notes, and cheques

donated by some of the richest banks in the City of London.

Das Meingold
(The Goldmine)

Said Lord Isaacs, who has done more than anyone else to assemble the sackloads of cash which now tower over Covent Garden, "This is a tribute not only to my rich friends but also to all the poor people who have contributed so generously through the National Lottery Fund. Together they have helped to put Britain right back at the centre of the financial world."

THE TODAY PROGRAMME
What You Missed

Sue McGhastly (for it is she): ...and with more news of that church massacre in South London, we have in the studio the Catholic priest Father O'Ted. Father?

O'Ted: Good morning, Sue.

McGhastly: Father O'Ted, now I know you weren't in the church at the time when this awful tragedy took place, but if you had been can you imagine what you might have seen?

O'Ted: Well, may I say first what a terrible shock and trauma this news has been to the whole Catholic community.

McGhastly: Yes, but what about the sword? Do you think you would have seen the assailant running up and down the aisles, slashing at terrified members of the congregation, including old-age pensioners and toddlers?

O'Ted: Well, Sue, as I say, I wasn't actually there.

McGhastly: Yes, but surely you can use your imagination. There you are, standing at the altar, and suddenly this maniac bursts in and starts hacking people to death. There's blood spurting everywhere, limbs flying across the pews. It must have been pretty terrible, mustn't it?

O'Ted: Yes, that's right, Sue.

McGhastly: And now, could I come to you, Jack Straw? Can I ask you, as Home Secretary, how long it will be before the Government imposes a long-overdue ban on Samurai swords? I mean, this terrible massacre would never have happened if these appallingly dangerous weapons were not easily available in the High Street.

Straw: Quite right, Sue. And I'm glad to announce that I'm going to introduce an emergency Bill to close all churches on Sundays, to ensure that a tragedy like this is never repeated. It's a crackdown on Samurai mass-murder. And we're serious about this.

McGhastly: Thank you, Home Secretary. And now, the weather with Sally Isobar. Sally, apparently there's going to be rain in Northern Ireland and Western Scotland, with snow on high ground, but slightly warmer in the south with occasional showers coming in later in the day?

Isobar: Thank you, Sue.

McGhastly: And now over to my colleague Jim Naughtie, whom I think is going to ask Jeremy Isaacs whether all these billion of pounds they've spent on the new Royal Opera House has been justified. And I suspect Lord Isaacs is going to reply "yes".

Naughtie: That's right, Sue.

Isaacs: Yes, Sue.

Sue Megalomaniac: And now, back to me (continues in same vein for several hours).

Christmas is coming,
Cherie's getting fat.
Please put a vote
In Tony's hat.

DAME MAGGIE'S TRIUMPHANT RETURN TO THE STAGE

by Our Showbiz Staff **Sir Ned Twinky**

IT DOES not sound a very promising role for one of the greatest theatrical stars of the millennium.

A mad old woman with a tattered old handbag and a weakness for the bottle decides to camp out on the lawn of a shy, inoffensive Yorkshireman and proceeds to make his life hell.

Yet Dame Maggie pulls it off spectacularly, with a bravura display of shouting, ranting and screaming abuse.

The unfortunate William Hague (played by Alan Bennett) does his best to cope with the antics of the crazed old lady at the bottom of his garden. But Dame Maggie (played by Margaret Smith) steals the show, as she did in the earlier version when her victim was the hapless John Major.

WHAT THE CRITICS SAID

"Wonderfully repulsive – a real theatrical monster."
E. Heath, BROADSTAIRS GAZETTE

"Dame Maggie is fantastic – theatrical Viagra."
Charles Spencer Moore, DAILY TELEGRAPH.

"Come back, Dame Maggie – all is forgiven."
Paul Johnson, SPANKS AND SPANKMEN.

Booking Now – *"The Lady Thatcher In The Van".*
Tickets available in all parts of the house.

 **AN ALTERNATIVE VOICE**

Cedric Spart, Co-Chair of the Neasden Gay Olympic 2001 Committee and Bronze Medallist in this year's Throwing the Tantrum *(shurely 'discus'? Ed)*

. . . Er the reaction to Sir Elton John's totally innocent dance routine with a group of boy scouts is utterly sickening and merely confirms once again the totally repressive nature of the heterosexual establishment who consistently try and link homosexuality with paedophilia when everybody knows perfectly well that just because you are gay does not mean you are interested in little boys as Sir Elton proved by his lighthearted and utterly amusing rendition of "It's a sin and a criminal offence" whilst fondling the semi-naked dancers in their tight uniforms er. . . er. . . the total and complete misrepresentation of this incident by the hetero-fascist media shows *(cont. p. 94)*

Anyone fancy a Bob-a-Job?

"Yes, it is rather good – a new chap called Wolfgang Muzak, I believe"

26

In the Courts

Day 94
Fugger vs. Freeloader

The case continued today

George Carphone QC *(acting for Mr Fugger)*: Mr Freeloader, if you would be so kind as to cast your mind back to the events of 1984 and in particular your special Winter Sleaze Break at the Writz Hotel in Paris.

Mr Freeloader: It's a lie!

Mr Fugger: It fuggin' well isn't!

Justice Cocklecarrot: Mr Carphone, I must ask you to restrain your client.

Mr Fugger: Don't you fuggin' try it Carfugger. Or you get no fuggin' fee!

Mr Carphone: I am indebted to you, Mr Fugger.

Mr Fugger: You certainly are…

Mr Cocklecarrot: Gentlemen, could we kindly get on with the matter in hand?

Mr Carphone *(Resuming his cross-examination)*: Mr Freeloader, do you recall what you ate for breakfast on the morning of March 2nd?

Mr Freeloader: It's a lie!

Mr Carphone: Do the words "grapefruit segments" refresh your memory at all, Mr Freeloader? And does the price of 40,000 francs per segment make the picture any less cloudy?

Mr Freeloader: You'll have to ask my wife.

Mr Carphone: I shall have that pleasure later but in the meantime I would be grateful if you would examine Bundle B.

Mr Freeloader: Is there any money in it?

Mr Cocklecarrot: There isn't any in mine.

Mr Fugger: That's because you don't fuggin' get any, until I win the fuggin' case.

(Laughter in court)

Mr Cocklecarrot: Mr Fugger, the court cannot tolerate any more of these outbursts.

Mr Fugger *(crying)*: I am just a poor working man who the Duke of Edinburgh has tried to murder on more than one occasion.

Mr Cocklecarrot: I see it is half past ten. Perhaps this is a suitable moment to adjourn for luncheon. This should allow Mr Fugger a few hours to recover his composure.

Mr Desmond Browne Nose OE, QC: Are you lunching at the Garrick today, M'Lud?

Mr Cocklecarrot: I am afraid that is Sub Judice.

Mr Browne: I'll see you there.

(The case continues)

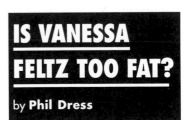

What the Freeloaders had for breakfast

15 Bottles vintage Krug champagne	100,000,000F
6 Bottles Chateau La Tour 1948	50,000,000F
1 Bowl Frosties	20,000F
1 Bowl Special K	30,000F
2 Slices brown toast with marmalade	25,000F
7 Lobsters in truffle sauce with caviar	200,000,000F
Confit of larks' tongues	700,000,000F
One boiled egg (with 'des soldats')	10,000 F
30,000 complimentary copies of the humorous magazine Punch	Free

TOTAL: **10 Billion Francs**

(service not included)

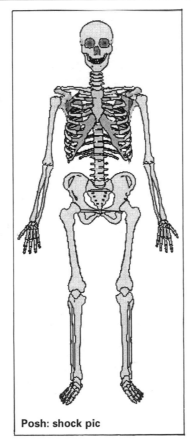

Posh: shock pic

IS POSH TOO THIN?

by Phil Plate

THIS IS the question that the whole world is asking after seeing this recent photograph of Victoria Beckham at a showbiz party.

Looking gaunt and fragile, the Spice Girl drew gasps from fans:

"She seems to have lost an awful lot of weight," said one. "She's just skin and bone," said another. "Or rather, just bone."

But Posh was having none of it. *(And that was just her dinner. Ed.)*

"These rumours about me being bulimic make me want to throw up," she told reporters. "I am very happy with my figure, ie 4 stone."

IS BECKHAM TOO THICK?

by Phil Plato

THIS IS the question that the whole world is asking after reading an interview with the footballer in OK Magazine. But Beckham was quick to play down worries about his recent thickness.

"I have always been thick," he said. "I may have got a bit thicker since having a baby. Or was that Victoria who did that? I can't remember."

IS VANESSA FELTZ TOO FAT?

by Phil Dress

THIS IS the question that the whole world *(That's enough questions. Ed.)*

"Not drinking the coffee, Dave?"

THE THREE AD MEN

POLLY FILLER

I DON'T want to sound hard-hearted but the next Romanian woman who pushes her grubby baby into my face on the Underground will get an earful from the famed Polly Filler tongue!

If there is one thing I cannot abide it is the spectacle of women using their children to try and make money.

As I explained to my toddler Charlie when he asked if he could give the poor lady his pocket money, "She is not a poor lady, Charlie, she is a cynical professional who is trying to exploit you." Charlie, having inherited his father's soppy genes, burst into tears which no amount of consoling by the nanny could stop.

His nose filled with snot and I thought he was going to have "an accident" right there on the train! He looked so funny that it was difficult not to laugh at him. I suppose he was a bit emotional because his guinea-pig had died and the useless Simon (briefly stirring himself from *Dwarf Darts from Melbourne* on *Sky Extreme 2*) had flushed it down the loo saying it was a burial at sea!

Charlie had wanted a full funeral in the garden and had written a rather embarrassing little poem which he wanted to put in the grave with the recently deceased "Fluffy". (His name *not* mine. I suggested, rather amusingly I thought, that the guinea-pig should be called "Euro Pig" instead! But the joke was somewhat wasted on Charlie.)

ANYWAY, there we were at Charing Cross with the tearful toddler bawling his eyes out with our new Chechnyan nanny blubbing along unhelpfully, all because of this selfish scrounger.

As I said to my fellow passengers on the tube, "If this so-called beggar woman really wanted some money, she could come and clean my toilet once a week."

Everyone seemed to agree with me and showed their support by getting out at the next stop and moving into another carriage whilst complaining loudly about "that ghastly woman with the child".

© Polly Filler.

WENCESLAS ATTACKED BY BLAIR
by Our Welfare Staff
Jon Snowman

AN ELDERLY Bohemian philanthropist was yesterday criticised for "a nanny state approach to welfare at Christmastime" by the Prime Minister.

According to reports, the rich, Czechoslovakian-born do-gooder had spotted an old man gathering winter fuel round about Boxing Day and had then personally distributed food and wine, assisted by a small child in his employ.

Said a furious Blair, "This was simply encouraging the old man to stay out in the snow looking for further hand-outs. Wenceslas did nothing to provide a long-term solution to the old man's problems in terms of reintroducing him into the Czech labour and community infrastructure."

THOSE SINN FEIN CABINET POSITIONS IN FULL

MARTIN McGUINNESS
(Education Secretary)
Main duties: Teaching people a proper lesson

BAIRBRE DE BRUN
(Health Secretary)
Main duties: Hospital admissions (after they've been taught that lesson)

Those New Northern Ireland School Rules In Full

1. Fighting in the playground is compulsory.
2. Any weapons brought to school will not be confiscated.
3. Anyone placed in detention will be let out immediately.
4. There will be no marching in the corridor.
5. The following sports will be played: Cross Country Gun Running, Baseball Batting, Hurling (Grenades).

(That's enough lessons – Ed)

CHRISTMAS MESSAGE

Peace on Earth, Goodwill to Men

NO!

EURO SOARS TO NEW LOW
Single Currency Plunges To New High

by Our Euro Is Marvellous Staff
Anatole Kaletsnotbebeastlyabouttheeurosky

CHAMPAGNE corks were popping in the capitals of euroland last night as the much-vaunted single European currency equalled the value of the once-mighty dollar.

When I spoke off the record to a very senior official of the European Central Bank (Mr E. Izzard), he told me: "Ze euro is marvellous. Whatever she does is just great.

"She go up – it's brilliant. She go down – it's even better. How unlike your stupid boring old pound which just stays the same all the time."

All I can say is that here in Europe I witnessed old-age pensioners dancing openly in the streets, as they gave three cheers for the titan of EU finances, Mr Wim Duisenberg, who said: "If the euro is a sound investment, then I'm a Dutchman."

BLAIR BELIEVES IN BEARDED SANTA FIGURE

by Our Christmas Staff
Phil Stocking

THE PRIME Minister hit out last night at the cynics who refused to believe in the jolly bearded figure known to children as St. Gerry.

Mr. Blair was furious at the suggestion that the hirsute philanthropist would not deliver his gifts of guns at Christmas or even in February.

HO-HO HOME RULE!

"Of course he will," said Mr. Blair. "No-one knows how St. Gerry and his helpers will do it, but it is one of the central mysteries of Christmas."

Bethlehem Times

— 25 December, 0 A.D. —

Yes! It's Peace On Earth!

by Our Christmas Staff **Jon Snowman**

THERE WAS widespread rejoicing last night at the glad tidings that heralded a new era of peace on earth and goodwill towards men.

Gerry Christmas

The Angels' announcement came after thousands of years of armed conflict around the globe and was widely welcomed as a significant breakthrough for humankind.

However, the mood of euphoria was somewhat tempered by the news that Mr. Martin McHerod was to be put in charge of childcare for the province of Judea. Critics point to Mr. McHerod's alleged involvement in the slaughter of various innocents and *(continued chapter 94, verse 37)*

SPECIAL *Private Eye's* MILLENNIUM SOUVENIR ISSUE

YES — IT'S 2000!
'I See Sun Rise On Kiritekanawa Islands'

by Our Man On The Meridian Line **Phil Space**

THE WORLD has seen nothing like it for 1000 years, or perhaps longer.

Today I saw with my own eyes the once-in-a-lifetime spectacle of the first sun of the new Millennium rising over the palm-fringed atoll of Kiritekanawa (formerly the Gilbert and George Islands).

As the first rays of millennial light pierced the low clouds over the Pacific horizon, a chorus of grass-skirted maidens specially flown in from New Zealand burst into their traditional song Aloha Dolly, only to be drowned out by the sound of hundreds of mobile phones ringing in the pockets of journalists as their editors rang to ask them where their copy was.

KEEP GOING, ED

Make no mistake, it was an awesome moment which none of us who were there will ever remember *(Surely "forget"? Ed.)*

No sooner had the ancient ritual chanting come to an end than the hundreds of Polynesian-style dancers rushed barefoot across the coral sand to a giant TV screen showing the fireworks over Sydney Harbour Bridge.

"Not half as good as the Eiffel Tower," they all cried in unison, as they *(cont'd. p. 94)*

HOW THE WORLD SAW IN THAT HISTORIC MILLENNIUM

Hong Kong: a spectacular firework display greeted revellers

Moscow: revellers were greeted with a spectacular fireworks display

Buenos Aires: revellers agreed they had never seen such a spectacular display of fireworks

Montreal: spectacular fireworks were greeted by revellers

Kinshasa: thousands of revellers were greeted by one firework

Grozny: thousands of revellers were greeted by a spectacular display of rockets laid on by the Russian army

● **More Firework Pictures – pages 8, 9, 10, 11, 12 etc.**

Copies of this historic issue are already collectors' items and are changing hands for hundreds of pounds.

Send off now for extra copies to pass on to your children and their children's children to put in their hamster cages *(surely "to cherish for ever"? Ed)*.

As seen in all papers

A New Dawn

AS A new millennium dawns on the anniversary of the birth of Christ and we reflect on the uncertainties of this rapidly changing world with its unending struggle between good and evil, the eternal question remains: Why the bloody hell was I made to queue for three hours with all the riff-raff just to get into the Dome where the champagne was tepid anyway. I mean, don't they know who I am?

2000
Zero Gravitas

by Andrew Lloyd-Motion
(To be sung to the tune of Auld Lang Syne)

This voice came into my head. "My God,"
It said. "It is the Millennium. And
As the Poet Laureate
I've got to write a poem about it.
I was making myself a cup
Of Nescafe at the time, in
The kitchen.
Through the window I saw a
Robin, singing with the sad music
Of the bird tribe.
"Hullo," I said, "would you like
Some of this rich tea biscuit?"
But he flew away, leaving the
Space on my window-sill
Empty. Just as one year flies
Away, leaving nothing in its place
Except another year. Another year,
Another century, another millennium,
Another cup of coffee.
How time flies!

Reprinted by permission of The Mail on Sunday £2000
(surely 2000 A.D.?)

To The Editor of the Daily Telegraph

Her Majesty And The So-Called Dome

SIR – No wonder Her Majesty looked so disapproving as she refused to cross hands during the singing of Auld Lang Syne. She was clearly expressing her contempt for Mr Blair's touchy-feely New Labour nonsense which the so-called Dome so eloquently symbolises.

SIR BUFTON TUFTON MEP
St Rasburg,
Dorset.

SIR – Whatever your ignorant correspondents may think, Her Majesty proved once again to be the only person in the entire Dome who was fully conversant with the correct procedure for the singing of Auld Lang Syne. As the Queen demonstrated, it is customary to sing the first verse merely holding hands with one's immediate neighbour and looking very bad-tempered. Only at the start of the second verse are the arms crossed. The words of this verse, with which only the Queen seemed familiar, are as follows:

Awa' wi' ye, ye whey-faced loon
We'll ha' nae truck wi' your silly doom.
Sae gang awa' ye sleekit beastie,
An' leave the rest o' us tae feastie! (Rabbi Burns attr.)

It was of course Queen Victoria who instituted the customary singing of this song at Balmoral at Hogmanay accompanied by a lone piper, and Her present Majesty has faithfully honoured this tradition until this year's travesty in the so-called Dome.
THE McMASSINGBERD
OF THAT ILK
Isle of Eigg-on-Toast,
Skye Sports.

SIR – The McMassingberd of McMassingberd is quite wrong to claim that the Queen crossed hands in the second verse of Auld Lang Syne, when she pointedly refrained from doing any such thing. Traditionally, participants only cross hands in the third verse, which the organisers of the so-called Dome did not even deign to include. The words of this verse, attributed to Bonnie Prince Charlie, are as follows:

You gang och doon yon bonnie glen,
Clags breeches brune and doon agane,
You hamish doch auld Donny Dewar,
And heave Lord Lairg into the sewer.

SIR JOHN FARQUHAR-SMITH
(Honorary Clan Chief of the Clan McFarquhar-Smith)
Stevenage, Herts.

From The Perkins Family

SIR – I think we can top the experience of the Pinkerton family of Ongar. Our family (including a 97-year-old great-grandmother and three toddlers under 2) set off from Trafalgar Square just after midnight and did not arrive home in Raynes Park until three days later. During this time we were not able to obtain access to a single public toilet, and were several times charged by mounted police busy searching for the killer of Jill Dando. No wonder *(cont'd. p. 94)*

Roll up! Roll up! It's the Big Flop!

Surely 'Top'?

101 Uses For A Dome

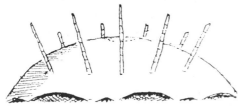

No.1 GM Crop-Testing Area

BRITISH COUPLE REACH DOME

by Philippa Page

HISTORY was made today when a British husband-and-wife team, Mike and Fiona Anorak, became the first couple ever to get through to the fabled Dome.

"We are tired but triumphant," said computer programmer Mike Anorak, 33. "We never thought we would make it, and there were many times when, frankly, we thought we would have to turn back and go home to Wallasey."

The couple began their epic, 37-hour trek when they left their semi-detached executive home on the John Lennon Estate at 9.37 last Tuesday morning.

This was their "Timetable of Achievement" in what they are calling "the toughest journey in the world":

9.46 am Virgin service to London cancelled owing to "train shortages". Couple take mini-cab to London.

5.15 pm Couple arrive at Jubilee Line station and board train for Dome.

6.24 pm Jubilee train leaves station.

6.25 pm Train returns to station due to points failure.

9.35 pm Now facing what they described as "intolerable conditions", the Anoraks, along with 17,000 other people, are stranded at Stratford station.

11.20 pm Anoraks finally join queue for entry to Dome. Interactive electronic sign tells them "Only 14 hours to wait".

1.26 am Mrs Anorak makes near-fatal mistake by joining queue for McDonald's "Millenniumburger Experience".

5.16 am Expedition hit by mystery food poisoning. Mrs Anorak tells her husband "I don't think I can make it. You go on without me," but Mike persuades her to struggle on.

10.15 am The Anoraks now only four miles from the centre of the Dome. In his diary Mike writes, "At last the end is in sight. We can just make out the spiky bits sticking out of the roof. It is an awesome sight."

3.31 pm Success! The Anoraks finally reach their goal and raise the Union flag.

3.38 pm Security staff eject couple from Dome saying "You've had your time. There's nothing to see. Get out!"

3.39 Special message of congratulation sent to Anoraks by Prime Minister Tony Blair, praising himself for his astonishing achievement.

ON OTHER PAGES

British couple reach bankruptcy – Mr and Mrs Hamilton "Delighted" **p. 94**

Those Domes – How They Shape Up
Comparison Of A Typical Day Out
by Samuel Taylor Nick Coleridge

	Pleasure Dome	Millennium Dome
Location	Easy to reach Xanadu	Inaccessible Greenwich
Nearest Transport	Handy for Alph, the sacred river	Hopeless connections to Thames and Jubilee Line
Organiser	Kubla Khan	Jennie Page
Best Feature	"Caverns measureless to man"	Giant pubic lice
Refreshments	Milk of paradise	McDonalds
Reaction of Snellgrove Family from Guildford	"Stately"	"Boring"

Conclusion: The Eye says "You'd have more family fun at Xanadu"

UPFRONTERS

MILLENNIUM DOME NEW YEAR PARTY SPECIAL!

☉ It's countdown to Y2K with **Richard**! And **Whiteley** so! Especially when the answer to the question "Who's with him?" is the delicious **Zenab Badawi**, the newsreader from Channel Phwoar!?!

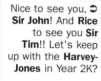

Nice to see you, ☉ **Sir John**! And **Rice** to see you **Sir Tim**!! Let's keep up with the **Harvey-Jones** in Year 2K?

♁ These three are having one **El-ton John** of a time! By **George**, I hope he's not taking the Michael out of Mrs Blair! Because she's the **Cherie** on the Y2 cake!

☉ What a **Stella** evening the Y2K has turned out to be! Especially when Miss **McCartney** has her designs on veteran comedy star **Leslie Phillips**!? Ding dong! Hello! What a carry on for Year 2K? *(You've done this one. Ed.)*

☉ Is **Denise** getting **Outen** about? And who's looking in your keyhole – don't be **Gross, man**, it's **Lloyd**! She's certainly something for the weekend! And Y2K not?!

Frying tonight!? ☉ **Stephen** certainly is, and we reckon he's Wilde about the gorgeous **Catherine**!? Give him an Oscar!? Talk about keeping up with the **Zeta Jones** at the big 2YK bash!? *(You've done this joke as well. Ed.)*

♁ Who's the **McQueen** of the 2KY Ball? Is it **Zoe** on his left or is it **Naomi** on his right? Or is it **Alexander** in the middle?! Watch out – the **Campbell** is coming!? Jingle **Balls**!?!

And, remember, 2YK is company, three's a crowd at the *(You're fired. Ed.)*

My Night Out At The Dome

by Dominic Lawson (aged 11½)

Yesterday we went to the Dome for our holiday treat. We put our best clothes on and we were really looking forward to it. But guess what? We only got stuck at the station for four hours.

What a total swizz! I got jolly batey, I can tell you!

© *Dome-nic Law-Zone, The Sunday Telegraph 2000*

A Taxi-Driver writes

Every week a well-known cabbie is asked to give his views on an issue of topical importance.

This week: **Dobbo Dobson** (Camden Cab Co. No. 2713)

BLIMEY, guv, see all those toffs having to queue up in the rain to get into the Dome? You had to laugh, didn't you? Ha ha ha! That Greg Dyke and co all dressed up in their penguin suits having to slum it with the riff-raff? Ha ha ha ha!

No, don't get me wrong, guv! I think it's a scandal, the treatment they got and no offence to all the ordinary people. No I've got a lot of time for the likes of Greg Dyke, that Roland Rat was brilliant. No I'm sorry about what I said earlier. Have this ride on me. Will you give me your vote guv?

I had that Simon Kellner in the back of the cab – blimey, only just squeezed him in!

*NEXT WEEK: **Andy Roberts** (Cab No. 9472) on why my mate Jonathan Aitken never done nothing wrong.*

"And when you started licking your bum I could've died"

Posh Admits 'Becks Loves My Thongs – Even Though I Cannot Thing'

By Our Domestic Staff Tharah Thands

THE DAILY TELEGRAPH can exclusively reveal that Spice Girl Victoria Beckham, known to her millions of fans as "Posh", went on television yesterday and said something very important to TV presenter Johnnie Vaughan.

On Other Pages

Big pix of Catherine Zeta Jones **2**

Train Crash In Norway **94**

Plus

Editorial: The Old Thongs Are The Besht by Bill Deedes

Britain's biggest-selling quality daily

HOGARTH REVISITED

Book Street

Video Lane

That Honorary Degree Citation In Full

SALUTAMUS MAUREENAM MOWLAMENSIS VULGARE "MO" POPULISSIMA MINISTERIA IN GOVERNMENTO ANTONINI BLAIRIS (DUX UNIVERSUS ET CETERA ET CETERA) CREATOR PACIS IN HIBERNIA BOREALIS ET AMICUS SANCTI GERALDO ADAMI SED INIMICUS TRIMBLI ET REVERENDO PAISLII DISMISSA AB BLAIRO IN ULTIMA HORA UT PROVIDARE IMPORTANTUM POSTUM PER PIETRO MANDELSONIO AMICO FAVORITTISIMO BLAIRENSIS (DUX UNIVERSUS ET CETERA ET CETERA) ET FURIOSISSIMA RETURNEBAT AD BRITANNICUM SIGNARE CONTRACTUM PER SCRIBENDO LIBRUM SENSATIONALEM CUM RUPERTO MURDOCHO ET RECEPIT CCCMLMLXXX DENARII ET DISSMISSA ERIT PROXIMO ANNO QUO POETA DICIT "AMO, AMASS, AFORTUNE".

© UNIVERSITATE DUNELMENSIS MXCM

SHOULD TAKI BE RETURNED TO GREECE?

by Our Antiquities Staff **Lord Elginandtonic**

THERE were renewed demands last night that Britain should hand back the world-famous Taki to Greece.

Taki was brought to London from Athens many decades ago by a bargain-hunting English aristocrat, Lord Henry Keswick, who wished to exhibit him in the pages of the Spectator as an example of classical Greek decadence.

BORIC COLUMNS

The call for the sending back of what one expert has described as "This disgusting pile of old rubbish," came from British art lovers who cannot stand the thought of the Taki remaining on these shores a moment longer.

But fierce opposition to the repatriation has come from his native Greece. "We have far too many of his sort here already," said a leading Athenian curator, "and you British can keep him.

"We understand that his condition has deteriorated badly since he has been in London. He is covered in white dust and his nose is missing."

"He is all slimy," said the distinguished expert, "and in his present state is no use to anyone."

Taki Takalotofcokupthenos is 2500 years old.

RUGBY STAR ACQUITTED SHOCK

by Our Court Staff **Rod Rage**

MR Jeremy Guscott, the international rugby player, was last week found to be "famous" by a jury in Bristol.

The England centre was accused of grievous bodily harm after an incident on a pedestrian crossing, but the jury decided that he was "clearly on television" and all the evidence pointed to him being "a celebrity".

They therefore agreed that Gaskett was beyond any reasonable doubt "pretty nippy over 25 metres" and reached a majority verdict of "guilty of scoring jolly good tries for England".

The court then rose to give Mr Blow-a-Gasket a standing ovation.

In a moment, we'll be talking about all the latest fashions for baby and how to cheer up those dreary old sausages. But first, a make-over for mister crocodile!

BREAKFAST IN BED WITH NORRIS

One hump or two?

Sunday Thanes

LADY MACBETH BREAKS DOWN IN COURT

"My husband is good man" – Shock Claim

by Our Court Staff **Joshua Rosencrantz**

THE wife of the controversial politician Mr Neil Macbeth today wept openly in the witness box when giving evidence for her husband, who has been accused of a multitude of offences.

"There is no way my husband could have murdered anyone," said Lady Christine Macbeth. "I went through his pockets every night and I never found a dagger in any of them."

She told the court how she and the accused had first met when they were members of the Young Feudalists Society at the University of Cawdor (formerly Glamis Polytechnic).

"I have stood by him through foul and fair," she said. There was laughter in court when she was asked by Mr Macduff QC, Counsel for the prosecution, "Which were you?"

Lady Macbeth continued to give evidence as to how her life had been ruined. "Neither of us can sleep," she sobbed, "and my husband has suffered from hallucinations over dinner."

"Would you like some water?" the judge asked. "No, thank you," she replied. "I only drink champagne."

The case continues.

CHANGING ROOMS

Well we've 24 hours - best get cracking

Hope they like it

This Year's Names

From The Rev. Jack Nutter

Sir, As is my custom at this time of year, I have made a tally of the most popular names ocurring in the Times Births' Column over the last Millennium. They are as follows:

Boys	Girls
Ethelred	Boadicea
Wayne	Posh
Darren	Scary
Peregrine Worsthorne	Mel
Becks	Petronella
Mohamed Al Fayed	Mrs Thatcher
Red Rum	Madonna
Red Ken	Polly Toynbee
Simon de Montfort	Mo
Simon Jenkins	Delia

Yours,
REVEREND JACK NUTTER,
The Vicarage, Duncountin, Nutts.

EXCLUSIVE SERIALISATION

ENGLAND'S 1000 BEST BORES

No. 94. St Simon, Jenkins

BUILT in 1943, St Simon's blooms over Wapping with its self-important façade and somewhat empty interior. We sense immediately an aura of overpowering tedium, as we penetrate the gloomier recesses of this forbidding edifice. It is a relief when our eye finally alights on his highly-decorative wife, the Blessed Gayle of Hunnicutt, who has worn well over the years. But there is no doubt that St Simon's is one of the outstanding bores of the last millennium.

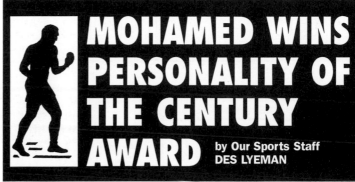

MOHAMED WINS PERSONALITY OF THE CENTURY AWARD

by Our Sports Staff **DES LYEMAN**

THE COVETED title of Most Unpleasant Personality of the Century was awarded after a unanimous vote to the heavyweight Egyptian tycoon, Mohamed Ali-Fayed.

There were tears as he stepped up to accept his trophy in recognition of his remarkable achievement in 1997 of bringing down the Tory Government in their third round.

Safety Deposit Boxing

Said one judge, "With his dirty below-the-belt fighting and his feeble Punch, Mohamed Ali-Fayed will go down in history as the undisputed King of the Bung."

Mohamed first came to prominence under the name Cashinus Hand, but changed his name to Mohamed Ali-Fayed in the hope of gaining British citizenship.

Courts Personality

He then beat the heavyweight German bully, Tiny "Tiny" Rowland, in a ten-round contest lasting a record 15 years. Known as "The Rumble in the Food Hall", Ali's victory established him as the undisputed infighter of his generation.

Fugilist

Even now everyone still knows and hates his catchphrase:

*"Float like a butterfly,
Sting like a fuggin' bee."*

Sadly, Mohamed is now suffering from Hamilton's Disease, causing him to tremble, burst into tears, and talk complete nonsense.

Of course I am sober. I can see two Jags

37

Nursery Times

Old Shoe Woman Arrested In Dawn Raid

by Our Nursery Crime Staff **Polly Putthetoynbeeon**

AN OLD woman, 75, who lives in a shoe, yesterday became the first victim of the government's new anti-smacking campaign.

She was arrested by armed police officers who broke into her shoe early yesterday morning, following a complaint from one of her many children.

Smacks Hastings

A police spokesman said "We received a hand-written note alleging that the old woman in question had so many children that she 'didn't know what to do'.

"However, this is no excuse for her subsequent actions — ie feeding them on broth without any bread, before whipping them soundly, and sending them to bed."

Following the old woman's arrest under S.28 of the new Abuse of Minors (Familial Situation) (Smacking) Regulations 2000, social workers removed the children to a nearby council home, where they could be properly abused by trained paedophiles.

The shoe is to be demolished.

European Nursery Rhymes

(From Mother Goosestep)

Old King Kohl
Was a Jerry old crook
And a Jerry old crook was he,
He called for his bribe,
And he called for his bung,
And he called for his fiddlers three hundred.

(Traditional)

DIANA 'A Fitting Memorial'

by Our Royal Staff **Phil Space**

A SPECTACULAR "Fountain of Drivel" two miles high is to be the centrepiece of the £10 million Diana Memorial Theme Park in west London.

The new park, which is to replace all the existing parks between Kensington Gardens and St James's Park, will consist of a continuous seven-mile walkway, connecting zones commemorating different aspects of Diana's life.

The trail will begin at Harvey Nichols and lead, via Lorenzo's Restaurant, down to the Chelsea Harbour Club, taking in on the way the barracks where James Hewitt served and the luxury apartment of her friend Dr Omar Sharif, and ending back in Knightsbridge at the department store Harrods.

QUEEN OF PARKS

The fountain itself will symbolise all the millions of words which have been spoken and written about the late Princess since she was taken from our midst towards the end of the last century.

LATE NEWS

Sinn Fein Condemns Terrorists

SINN FEIN today condemned the bombing of a hotel in Belfast by a group calling themselves The Continuity IRA.

"These people are a small unrepresentative group who are attempting to dictate the political process by the use of terrorism. But enough of us." *(Reuters)*

"Mind you, the gardens need it"

THAT WAKEHAM HOUSE OF LORDS PLAN

1. Number of peers to be dramatically reduced to 550.

2. Elected peers to be phased in over the next 1000 years.

3. Women peers to constitute not less than 30% and not more than 100% of assembly.

4. Not all peers to be members of House of Lords.

5. Bishops to remain in chamber provided they agree with abolition of Clause 28.

6. Law Lords to remain in chamber provided they have heard of The Beatles.

7. Gay peers to constitute not less than 78% Riboflavin (Vitamin E).

8. Report by Lord Wakeham to be so incomprehensible that Government can shelve it and continue to appoint whoever it chooses.

9. Er...

10. That's it.

© Lord Wakeham-up-it's-time-to-go-home

A WEST London man yesterday scooped the £6 million jackpot in the BBC's popular game show *Who Wants To Be A Director-General?*

These are the seven questions which made Mr Greg Dyke, 57, the richest man in TV history:

1. Would you like to be Director-General?
Yes/No/Don't Know/Maybe.
Correct Answer: Yes.

2. Which popular TV character is called Roland?
Roland Morse/Roland Rat/Two Fat Rolands/Joanna Lumley.
Correct Answer: Roland Rat.

3. Do you renounce Birt and all his works?
Congregation: I do.

4. Do you have any shares in Granada Television, the BBC's main competitor?
Yes/No/Maybe/You'll Have To Talk

To My Solicitor.
Correct Answer: Pass.

At this point the questions became more difficult, and a plainly nervous Mr Dyke began sweating visibly in front of 15 million licence-payers.

5. Do you think you should be allowed to hold onto these shares?

After a long pause, during which he turned bright red and fingered his non-existent beard, Mr Dyke asked "Can I phone a friend?"

He then rang Sir Christopher Bland, his old colleague at London Weekend Television, who now has a new job as Chairman of the BBC.

"Hullo, Chris. I don't have to sell these shares, do I?"

Sir Christopher replied, "Not if no one knows about them. No, definitely not."

But then came the even more testing sixth question:

6. If the public find out about your shares after you've been appointed, do you think you will look:
Shifty/Dodgy/Greedy/A Figure Of Moral Probity?

At this point, Mr Dyke turned to the audience and asked them for their opinion.

They all shouted "Dodgy", which was the correct answer.

Mr Dyke then faced the seventh and final question:

7. Now that you've been caught out, do you propose to sell your shares immediately?
Yes/No/It's All Very Complicated/You're Only Asking This Because The Murdoch Media Are Running A Vendetta Against Me.

Correct Answer: Bring back Lord Reith.

BIRT'S AUTOBIOGRAPHY
THAT TRILOGY IN FULL

—VOLUME ONE—
The Years of Rationalisation

The sensational story of the inter-departmental reorganisation that took the BBC infrastructure into the management vortex.

—VOLUME TWO—
The Coming of Producer Choice

The amazing never-before-told story of how Lord Birt's revolutionary introduction of mould-breaking accounting procedures sent shock waves through every strata of the BBC Directorate.

—VOLUME THREE—
The Digital Challenge

The extraordinary saga of one man's mission to embrace the new international standard of milli-pixel-per-nanosecond On-line Digital Reception.

Offers invited in the region of 3 or 4 pence for this Epoch-Making Series (shortly to be turned into a 100-part television drama and shown on BBC Choice at 3 o'clock in the morning).

All desperate publishers should apply at once to London's leading literary agent: Curtis Bore, W1.

EU ATTACKS HAIDER'S 'DISGRACEFUL VIEWS'

by Our Brussels Staff **Dick Tatte**

EUROPEAN Union chiefs were today united in condemning the leader of the Austrian Freedom Party for what they called his "unacceptable political opinions".

Said one spokesman, "Herr Haider has openly admitted that he does not admire the European Union and has made no secret of his dislike of the Commission. This is disgraceful."

He continued angrily, "We don't mind him being a fascist and a Nazi apologist, but to claim that the EU has not been good for employment — it is an outrage!"

Monsieur Gerbil
An Apology

WHEN we issued a press release on the inspired choice of Jean-Claude Gerbil, 32, as the new managing director of the Millennium Dome Experience plc, we may have inadvertently given the impression that Monsieur Gerbil was in some way the saviour of Euro-Disney, and that he had personally been responsible for reversing the fortunes of the once ailing French theme park. Our précis of his CV may have added to this confusion with its claims that the 27-year-old Frenchman had:

● **designed the Channel Tunnel;**
● **built the Pompidou Centre in a week;**
● **erected the Eiffel Tower with his bare hands;**
● **made love to thousands of incredibly beautiful French women while translating Proust.**

We now realise, after reading the Daily Telegraph, that M. Gerbil had not in fact been responsible for any of the above, and that he was in fact an unemployed 500 francs-a-week car park attendant from Limoges, whose greatest achievement was to institute the new one-way traffic flow system from the N274 to the Snow White's Olde English Pub toll-booth.

We further accept that former colleagues who described M. Gerbil as "a brilliant impresario" and "one of the greatest organisational geniuses of the late 20th Century" were talking about someone else. We would like to apologise to the British public for any distressing waste of money this confusion may have caused, while at the same time we would like to confirm our complete faith in M. Gerbil's ability to make the Dome the undoubted success it already is.

Issued by Lord Forkbender, Chairman of the Millennium Experience Not Needed Company

---

Telegraph Exclusive

'I Was The First Man On The Wheel'
by W.F. Deedes

IT WAS with a sense of mounting awe and excitement that I approached the famous wheel. It had taken 2 years to construct and had encountered early technical problems but suddenly here it was in all its glory, ready to go!

Designed by Ug and his team of cave dwellers, the wheel is every bit as impressive as the hype suggests.

It rolls, it spins, it rotates. It is a modern miracle. Standing on it you can gaze out at the glories of Cro-Magnon civilisation and see the dinosaurs grazing peacefully in the swamp below. Mark my words, the wheel is here to stay. In my view it is the best thing since they invented fire last week.

© Bill Deedes, 3004 B.C.

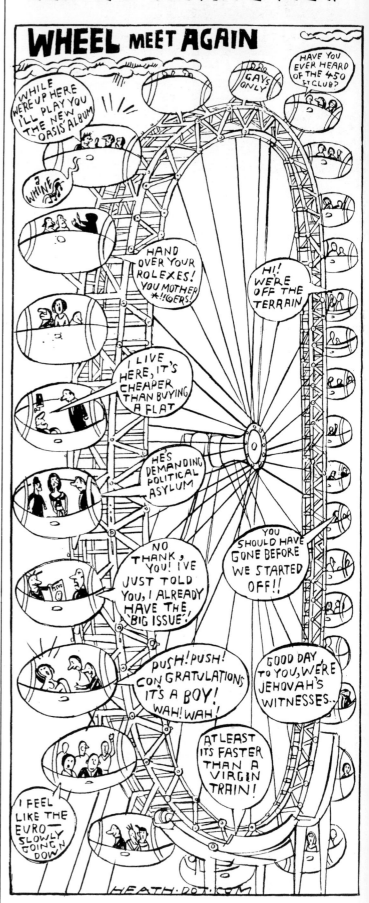

NO COVER-UP — IT'S OFFICIAL

by Our Cover-Up Staff **P.D. O'Phile**

IN HIS 2000 page report *Something Must Be Done*, the former High Court Judge Sir Ronald Waterdown makes it clear that although there was a clear cover-up of the decade-long history of abuse of hundreds of children in Welsh residential homes, this was not necessarily proof that there was some sort of cover-up.

Sir Ronald Waterdown was at pains to stress that although the social services, the local councils and the police were centrally involved in the scandal, the fact that they did nothing to stop it did not necessarily mean that they were in some way attempting to cover it up.

While Sir Ronald commended Mrs Alison Whistleblower for her attempts over 15 years to alert the relevant authorities to what was going on, he found that her sacking by her bosses and the subsequent attempt to smear her name with the full co-operation of the police did not in itself constitute proof of a cover-up.

Sir Ronald Waterdown emphasised that although officials of the social services, the councils, the police and the Welsh Office were obviously to blame for the scandal remaining hidden for so long he was not saying that those individuals had attempted to cover it up.

Sir Ronald Waterdown is 74.

"There's a fuck of a lot of cloud out to the west, so later it's going to piss down"

C4 WEATHER

Nursery Rhymes For Today

The Wheel on the Thames goes round and round.
Round and round,
Round and round.
The Wheel on the Thames goes round and round.
But nobody goes to the Dome.

(Trad.)

(and all other papers)

IT MUST NOT HAPPEN AGAIN

The report by Sir Ronald Waterhouse on the so-called North Wales paedophile affair makes very disturbing reading... appalling catalogue... neglect... betrayal of trust... physical and sexual abuse... innocent victims... appalling catalogue... need for tighter regulations... supervisory mechanisms... complaints procedures... something must be done... must never happen again... no time to read report... will this do?

POLLY FILLER

ON THE FLU

THERE's an epidemic in our household – but it's not flu, it's malingering! Or male-lingering as I call it! Because there's no such thing as flu, just men with colds and a pathetically low pain threshold! Take Simon (you're welcome to him sister!). The first sign of a temperature above 104 and he's lying in bed moaning and begging me to ring the doctor. And he's got wheezing and coughing to annoy me down to a fine art.

He's even pretending he's too ill to watch Kayak Racing from Winnipeg on Euro Sport. But he's fooling no one – except the gullible doctor who said he should be admitted to hospital as soon as possible.

To make matters worse, the new male au-pair Milos has gone back to Slovakia claiming that he was too ill to work ("flu" again!) and that he stood a better chance of treatment in Bratislava. Thanks a lot, Milos, and if you're reading this, you're fired.

Who said male nannies were much better than women? *(You in your last column. Ed.)*

SO, HERE I am trying to nurse the toddler Charlie, who has adopted male behavioural patterns early and is lying on his bed coughing and whingeing about so-called "flu"! And how much sympathy do I get? None whatsoever.

I've got to juggle all this childcare with writing a column, going to the gym and having lunch with a fashion PR.

And do my parents help?

I rang home yesterday demanding a bit of emergency relief only to find my mother droning on about my father getting flu and having an air ambulance whisking him off to Manchester in the middle of the night!

Men – they are such big babies! Next week someone else will be writing this column and I'll be having a well-deserved week's "flu" in the Bahamas.

See you.

© Polly Filler

FLU WHAT A SCORCHER!
60-70-80-90 (per cent of newspapers are filled with flu)

by Our Flu Staff **Sydney Virus**

BRITAIN is paralysed, according to experts, since the most severe outbreak of pieces about flu since the great Flu Story Epidemic of last year.

The symptoms are all too familiar weak storylines, fever-pitch writing and swollen headlines.

Add to this a nationwide shortage of stories and you have an epidemic of *(continued in 94% of the paper)*

WOTALOTIGOT!

HAPPY Piers Moron, 34, is laughing all the way to the Blank!

Thanks to yet another brilliant share tip from your Mirror City tipsters (who have sadly been sacked this week).

One day Piers was just an ordinary newspaper editor struggling along on £300,000 a year.

The next day he read the Mirror's share tips and became an overnight millionaire.

"It will not change my way of life," said a jubilant Piers. "I will go on editing the Mirror even though everyone thinks I should resign."

And Piers's boss Sir Victor Blank-Cheque is right behind him.

"I am delighted Piers has agreed to carry on working despite his good fortune," he said.

Piers was not the only lucky winner. He was part of an office syndicate, along with his deputy-editor, the City staff and most of the other journalists.

Between them, they received a record pay-out of £1 million.

YOUR PROBLEMS

Miriam
THE ADVICE COLUMN YOU CAN TRUST

Dear Miriam...
I AM 34 and I have a real problem getting my shares up. What do you advise?
PM, Canary Wharf.

Dear Piers...
THERE'S something new on the market that's just what you're looking for!

It's called Viaglen, and it works wonders. Buy a large packet, and watch your shares shoot up – and stay up!
Miriam.

Dear Miriam...
Do you think three-in-a-bed is wrong? Just recently my friend and I were duped by a long-time lover, and the very same day we got into bed with a very kind Egyptian gentleman.

He's very generous and gives us lots of presents. Is this wrong?
Yours, Anil Intercourse and James Knobswell

Dear Anil and James...
LOOK, don't be embarrassed! We've long gone past the days when people thought having money with each other was wrong!

Go with the flow – and make money with your new Egyptian sugar daddy.
Yours,
Dr Miriam Stoppaford.

Tomorrow: We banked 5 times a night – should we be ashamed?

ANDY CAPPITALIST

HELLO PET!

HAVE YOU BEEN WHERE I THINK YOU'VE BEEN?

YES, HAVING LUNCH WITH MY STOCKBROKER!

MEN! THEY ONLY THINK ABOUT ONE THING – MONEY!

THE STORY THEY TRIED TO GAG BY THE WOMAN THEY ARE CALLING 'NANNY JUDAS'

Chapter One

I SHALL never forget the day I first met Mr and Mrs Blair. They were a very nice couple with very nice children. "You are going to be our nanny," they said. "We hope you will be very happy with us."

Chapter Two

I WAS the Blairs' nanny! How happy I was. Our address was Number Ten, Downing Street, because Mr Blair was Prime Minister of England. And I was his nanny!

Chapter Three

MR BLAIR had a very nice friend called Mr Mandelson who speaks very quietly and has very nice manners. Once he came round and asked me for a bottle of pink champagne. "I'm celebrating a bit of luck," he said. "I've just bought a nice big house."

Chapter Four

ONE DAY a very important man came to the house. He was the Prime Minister of America. He had a funny accent and was very nice to all the ladies.

Chapter Five

EVERYONE I meet here is very nice. Unfortunately, I am not, so I'm off to the Mail on Sunday to sell them my story. "Can you spice it up a bit?" the nice Mr Peter Wright said. "No," I said. "Never mind," he told me. "It's not very interesting but I'll put it in any way." What a nice man.

Chapter Six

A VERY nice cheque arrived.
(To be continued)

BLAIR NANNY SHOCK

How dare she peddle feeble stories about me to the press?

That's my job

"Belinda, will you make me the happiest man in the world and divorce me?"

KenPyne

MARY POPPINS SPILLS BEANS

by Our Home Affairs Staff
Dick Van Dyke

IN what has been described as the most outrageous breach of confidentiality in the history of domestic service, a former nanny to the Banks family has sold her story to Walt Disney for an undisclosed seven-figure sum.

Mary Poppins, although claiming to get on well with the family, gives intimate details of their private life.

"Mr Banks is a wet, ineffectual man, only interested in his career, who does not spend enough time with his children," she writes.

SUPERTONYLOVELYCHERIECAMPBELL-ISATROCIOUS

But her scorn is reserved for Mrs Cherie Banks, whom she describes as "an ardent feminist, more committed to women's's issues than looking after her children".

Her story is filled with humorous anecdotes about their chimney-sweep friends and indiscreet descriptions of Mr Banks' office, but the Banks family are furious at the disclosures and last night sought a high court injunction to stop Poppins and her ghost writer, P.L. Travers, cashing in on these revelations.

Said Mr Banks, "You can't even go and fly a kite nowadays without it ending up on screen."

David Tomlinson is 81.

PROFILE

ALI F THE NEW COMEDY SENSATION

EVERYONE WAS laughing at the antics of the hysterical Ali F, Britain's newest and funniest comic. With his ridiculous accent and humorous catchphrases ("Fuggin conspiracy, innit?") Ali F has become the comedy cult of the Millennium.

Ali F (real name Mohamed Al Fayed) pretends to be a British citizen and has hilarious encounters with the great and the good.

In one classic encounter he accuses a baffled Prince Philip of being "a fuggin' murderer". In another he asks a confused Jack Straw why he can't have "a fuggin' passport". In the best skit of all he takes on Tory MP Neil Hamilton and cons him into asking dodgy questions for him in Parliament!

"Ali F is beyond satire," said top comedy producer Toppo Thompson of *The 11 Viewers Show*. "In the great tradition of British Comedy we laugh at him rather than with him."

'PLEASE LET ME DIE'
Lord Longford's Shock Plea

by Charles Moors-Murderers

THE 112-year-old Labour peer Lord Longford has been incarcerated in the House of Lords for most of his adult life.

Every day his routine is the same. He writes letters to the Times asking for the release of Myra Hindley and Ian Brady.

But now he has had enough, and is pleading with the authorities to be allowed to die in peace and dignity.

PACKIN-EM IT IN

Yesterday his oldest friend Miss Hindley said "I have known Frank for many years, and he is utterly sincere in his beliefs. He is a devout Catholic and during his time inside has made genuine efforts to better himself, by writing hundreds of books and becoming a Knight of the Garter.

"But now this poor old man has had enough. And all he asks is to be allowed to slip away live on Question Time, while answering a question on the Moors Murderers."

Lord Longlife is 342.

On Other Pages

"Please Let Me Die But In Chile" — General Pinochet's Shock Plea

---

In Today's Ghouldian

Exclusive extracts from the Rusbridger Letters in G2

"**I** WAS naïve and foolish and when Myra Hindley came into my life I was instantly attracted to the possibility of putting in long and graphic accounts of disgusting serial killings in the hope of titillating my supposedly right-on readers. And once I started serialising I couldn't stop."

In tomorrow's Ghouldian Rusbridger reveals how he was "only obeying orders" to put in a lot of stuff about Adolph Eichmann.

*The*Ghouldian Urghh!

Showing Off With Hensher

Each week the popular Indescribably-boring columnist Philip Hensher shares his unrivalled knowledge of the arts with readers.

SITTING at my corner table in Spanko's last week with Oofy and Crispin *(Didn't you do the gay lifestyle bit last time? Ed.)* I found myself recalling the long hot summer of 1981 when, at the age of four, or was it five, I first read Proust. Could it have been the Scott-Moncrieff translation or had Terence Kilmartin produced his dazzling volumes by then? I really can't remember. This led me, as perhaps I might have anticipated, to think of Berlioz. Why is it that, unlike myself, the dreary know-nothings who administer contemporary culture don't listen to Berlioz? Is it simply that their sensibilities are somehow untuned to the vertiginous switchback ride of his aesthetic?

Meanwhile, to my horror, I find that some rubbishy book for children (urghh!), almost as shockingly bad as the ghastly C.S. Lewis, has been short-listed by the Whitbread Prize, and may even beat David Cargs seventeen volume 3,938 page masterpiece on Berlioz's early years. It really is time for literary London to grow up. *(cont. p. 94)*

NEXT WEEK: How I bumped into Mike Tyson in the Selfridge's lingerie department.

"Not very busy then, Wadsworth?"

STAR TREK: THE NEXT GENERATION

Knock me up, Scotty!

SELLAFIELD LEAK SHOCK

by Our Nuclear Staff **Ray De Ation**

THE Government is to set up an enquiry into how a damaging leak of information about Sellafield safety occurred – threatening the jobs of hundreds of BNFL managers.

It is not yet known what caused the leak, but experts say it is nothing to worry about.

Said one, "There is no cause for alarm. Everything is under control. A report got out, but it has now been firmly denied. It will not happen again."

THE OBSERVER

Robert McCrummy

ANYONE who fails to discern that the translation of Beowulf by Seamus Heaney (published by my old firm of Faber and Favour) is much better than the feeble Harry Potter oeuvre is not merely a philistine, but is probably an anti-Catholic bigot and member of the Orange Order as well. Perhaps only the most intelligent observers of the literary scene like myself can see this clearly, but it is very obvious to those of us who have any sort of educated taste that the Potter-loving bourgeoisie are no better than illiterate neanderthals *(That's enough Whitbread. Ed.)*

So. Farewell then…

RIP
CHARLES
SHULTZ

CHINA TO JOIN EU

by Our Eurovision Staff
EURO'PHIL SPACE

THE Republic of China is the latest nation to join the ever-lengthening queue of applicants for EU membership.

The move was welcomed by EU President Romano Prodi who said "China has long been part of Europe. It is only natural that the EU should enlarge to take in countries such as Afghanistan, Zimbabwe and Chile, who are becoming increasingly aware of the wonderful benefits of belonging to a European superstate."

All China has to do to qualify for full membership is to buy 2000 billion euros on the money market, and agree to vote against Britain in all debates.

Mr Robin Cook joined President Prodi in welcoming the entry of China, North Korea and Iran into the EU, saying "They will be welcome allies in our ethical struggle against the Nazi hordes in Austria, led by their hated Führer Adolf Haider."

Stop Press

CHINA TO APPLY FOR 10 BILLION EUROS IN REGIONAL FUNDING

(Reuter)

CAPTAIN OF TITANIC TO BE HONOURED

by Our Political Staff
Dome Jennie Page

THE Prime Minister is to award honours to all those responsible for the successful sinking of the Titanic, it is revealed today.

Top of the list is Captain Bob Ayling who becomes a Life Peer (Posthumous) in the Queen's Birthday Honours List for his skill in launching the Titanic and guiding it safely into the waiting iceberg.

Also honoured is chief stewardess and entertainment officer Miss Jennie Page who becomes a Life Baroness (Dame Dome) for her supervision for the queues for the lifeboats and the band playing "Abide With Me" to an empty ballroom.

These appointments follow the recent life peerage awarded to John Birt, the pilot of the Hindenberg for his organisational skills in bringing the airship crashing to the ground in a ball of fire.

"Love the new tailplane..."

"There's never an institutionalised racist around when you need one!"

GPs TO BE BANNED

Government To Act

by Our Political Staff
Ron Knee-Jerk

THE Government has been quick to respond to MPs' demands for an immediate ban on all GPs, following the horrifying mass-murders by Cheshire doctor Harold Shipman.

"A tragedy like this must never be allowed to happen again," said a Downing Street spokesman, "and the only way to guarantee this is to ensure that all these highly dangerous doctors are taken out of circulation as soon as possible."

Never Again

The Government plans to introduce its Dangerous Doctors (How To Show That We Are Doing Something In The Wake Of This Tragedy) Bill early in the next session.

It has been estimated that there are currently over 20,000 GPs in practice, and every one of them, MPs were warning last night, is "potentially lethal".

Under the proposed legislation all GPs will be given 28 days to hand themselves in to the nearest police station.

A Doctor Writes
(You Off)

AS A Doctor, I am often asked, "Doctor, how many patients have you killed recently?"

The simple answer is: "Just sit down in that chair, and I'll give you a little injection."

© A. Murderer MM

TV Highlights

PICK OF THE DAY – Best Murder Mystery
BBC 9.00pm
The Case Of The 150 Dead Old Ladies
(in three parts)

WHEN hundreds of elderly women in the sleepy Cheshire town of Hyde are found dead in mysterious circumstances, it only takes seven years for Inspector Knacker *(Surely Morse? Ed.)* to notice that something is wrong. Luckily, one of the old ladies' relatives solves the case for him, bringing the family doctor to justice.

Eye Rating: *Worrying*

Lookalikes

Archole   **Enfield**

Sir,

I have noticed the similarity between those two great impressionists Jeffrey Archer and Harry Enfield. Jeffrey's jolly cockney looks rather similar to Harry's annoying "You don't want to do that" character. Obviously Jeffrey should have taken some of that advice!

PETER CHADBURN,

Via e-mail.

Putin   **Renard**

Sir,

I wonder if any of your readers have noticed the alarming resemblance between Mr Vladimir Putin, acting president of Russia, and "Renard", the Russian nuclear terrorist villain of the latest James Bond movie? Bearing in mind the recent revision of Russia's nuclear defence strategy, is there something we (and M) should be told?

Yours etc,
HADLEY,

Via e-mail.

Tesco girl   **Beckett**

Sir,

I wonder if any readers of your esteemed organ knows of family ties between Margaret Beckett, the gorgeous pouting leader of the House, and the bean-faced Tesco Personal Finance girl. I wonder if they are both dreaming of imminent retirement days on the beach. I think we should be told.

Yours aye,

ALICK WHITFIELD,

London SW10.

Winston   **Frayling**

Sir,

Son of Groucho moustaches, a certain smugness and spectacles — what else do our Lord Winston of the Stethoscope and Love-to-be-a-Lord Prof Frayling of the Royal College of Art and dome matters have in common?

A curious ENA B. RUSHTON,

London W1.

Dimmock   **Brockovich**

Sir,

Is buxom biopic babe Erin Brockovich related to buxom babybio babe Charlie Dimmock? I think Alan Titchmarsh should be told.

Sincerely,
JOHN DOCHERTY,

Paisley.

Tam Dalyell   **Chris Evans**

Sir,

These men are surely related.

F. EVANS,

Brighton.

Cartman   **Prescott**

Sir,

Is John Prescott by any chance related to South Park's "Cartman"?

Yours Faithfully,
Steve Crowley,

Orpington, Kent.

Cilla   **Marie**

Sir,

Has anyone noticed the similarity between Our Cilla and Our Marie [Lloyd]?

JERRY TURNER,

Westgate-On-Sea, Kent.

Hulk   **Jagger**

Sir,

Does Mick Jagger's agent realise his client is moonlighting? I think he should be told.

Yours faithfully,
MARTIN BOOTH,

Langport, Somerset.

George   **Brenda**

Sir,

A shot of Brenda enjoying herself on duty in Yorkshire the other day irresistably calls to mind another royal profile. It's George III by James Gillray in 1795.

Are they in some way related?

Yours historically
JOHN WARDROPER,

London N1.

Young **Toksvig**

Sir,

Is the stonewalling in the Lords over Section 28 connected to the resemblance between lesbian comedienne Sandi Toksvig and Baroness Young?

Yours,
OWEN MASSEY,

Loughborough, Leics.

Branson **Wise Man**

Sir,

Could this be Richard Branson featured as a gift-bearing wise man on La Sagrada Familia, Barcelona?

CLAIRE HENLEY & SIMON GROGAN,

Address unknown.

Mr Pringle **Seaman**

Sir,

Have any of your readers noticed the remarkable similarity between England goal keeper David Seaman, and Mr Pringle, the popular cocktail snack character? Is their facial hair by any chance related?

Yours,
D. Coleman,

Wembley.

Dipsy **Princess**

Sir,

Get ahead, get a hat – was this Princess Michael at Westminster Cathedral this week – or Dipsy of the Teletubbies?

Yours truly,
WENDY MOORE,

Hockley, Essex.

Yoda **Fayed**

Sir,

I have recently noticed the similarity between the alien Yoda from Star Wars and the alien owner of Harrods and proprietor of Punch. Which one has the best chance of British citizenship?

Yours,
PETER BRADLEY,

Kettering, Northants.

Sun Editor **Mr Potato Head**

Sir,

Have you noticed the amazing similarity between Sun Editor David Yelland and Mr Potato Head? Are they related? I think we should be told.

NAME & ADDRESS WITHHELD.

Hall **Ciccione**

Sir,

I'm sure all your readers will have noticed the amazing similarity between La Hall and La Ciccione. Do they share some mutual dark roots, I wonder?

Yours,
LOUIS HELLMAN,

London W3.

Sting **Archer**

Sir,

Have any of your readers noticed the remarkable similarity between well-known party host Jeffrey Archer and pop singer Sting? Are they by any chance related?

JOHN HOWSON,

Colchester, Essex.

Austin **Andrew**

Sir,

Reading an article on Tim Rice, I was very struck by the similarity between Andrew Lloyd Webber as a young man, and Austin Powers. I wonder if your readers would agree.

Yours faithfully,
KAREN ALLAN (Ms),

Dundee.

Smith **Dobson**

Sir,

Has anyone noticed the similarity between Captain Smith of Titanic fame and Frank Dobson, Labour mayoral candidate?

Yours,
TERRY GRAYSHON,

Via e-mail.

Clunes **Eliot**

Sir,

I couldn't help noticing the striking resemblance between T.S.Eliot and badly behaved man Martin Clunes.

Are they by any chance related? I think we should be told.

Yours sincerely
P.Brundish,

Bicester, Oxon.

Gore **Lewinsky**

Sir,

If anyone notices the resemblance of Al Gore's wife to Monica Lewinsky, could it blow his chances of getting the top job?

Regards,
GARETH WILLIAMS,

Via e-mail.

DICTATOR 'UNFIT TO REMAIN IN BRITAIN'

by Our Diplomatic Staff **Chile Cooper**

DOCTORS today certified the former British leader Mrs Thatochet is "unfit" to stay any longer in Britain on the grounds that she is "completely senile".

Her conduct, they conclude, has become irrational and embarrassing. Not only did she give General Pinochet a plate under the impression that he was Sir Francis Drake, but she even supported Lord Archer in his campaign to become Lord Mayor.

The doctors recommend that the hated despot is shipped immediately to secure accommodation in the Falkland Islands where she can be sure of a hero's welcome from a grateful population (Sid and Doris Penguin).

A spokesman for the dictator,

Mr Charles Moore, said: "She has suffered enough. It is now her only wish to be leader of the Tory Party again." *(Surely "retire with dignity"? Ed.)*

BBC ATTACKS CHURCH OF ENGLAND

by Our Religious Staff
Sir Clifford Longley-Richard

THE Church of England is accused of sidelining religion in a shock report compiled for the BBC. Sir Greg Dyke accuses the church of "trivialising important issues" and "dumbing down the content of services".

Carey In The Community

"All they do is talk about sex and gays. There's no attempt to deal with the real issues of religion at all."

An angry Archbishop of Canterbury hit back saying, "We have to appeal to all sections of the community and in particular to young people. If this means changing our methods of presentation and placing more emphasis on pop music, then so be it."

Joan Bakewell is 108.

This Week's Recipe	2. Leave there for 12 years until Bakewell boils over.
How To Make A Bakewell Tart	**3.** Remove from television and allow to simmer gently.
1. Put her programme on very late at night.	© Delia Smith

THE DAILY TELEGRAPH

Mind Your Own Business, Bishop!

Says **Dr Germaine Greer**, the Voice Of Reason

THE so-called Bishop of Rochester is talking through his tiny little mitre. In a disgraceful outburst, he has told us that married people should have children. His views are a combination of lamebrainedness, illiteracy and pathetic eagerness to see himself in the news which is so characteristic of myself. *(Surely "The Church of England"? Ed.)*

How dare this married man with the statutory 2.4 kids presume to lecture single childless women like myself on the subject of the family?

Why doesn't he mention the many men who murder their wives and children every day. That is the sort of thing he ought to be preaching about. What a bastard, like all men.

DR GERMAINE GREER,
The Old Coven,
Broom St. Ick,
Cambs.

DAILY TUDORGRAPH

MAFTER THOS. CRANMER RUDELY ASSAILED BY YE MAD MAID OF CAMBRIDGE

YE Archbishop of Canterburie, Mafter Cranmer, hath come under heavie fire for his views on Holie Matrimonie, as exprefsed in his new beft-feller Ye Booke of Common Prayer.

For, saith Cranmer, this holie institution is "ordained for ye procreation of children". "Come off it, your Grace," writeth Miftress Greer, ye fo-called "Mad Maide of Ye Fens" in ye Daily Tudorgraph. "What doth he knowe about fuch matters? He deserveth to be burned at ye ftake." *(Continued 1594)*

BRILLO NEW HAIRSTYLE SHOCK

BIG CHIEF RUNNING JOKE

> I'm really hoping to squaw

NEWSNIGHT
20th Anniversary Special
(Paxman Interviews Paxman)

Paxman: So, Jeremy, twenty years in the same job. Time to pack it in, wouldn't you say?

Paxman: Er... well, I think we've tried...

Paxman: Oh, come off it. It's all pretty predictable, isn't it? We've all had enough of you.

Paxman: No, I think that the programme still...

Paxman: But nobody watches it. It's on too late and it's full of bores.

Paxman: No, that's unfair...

Paxman: Answer the question. Is it full of bores?

Paxman: Let me begin by...

Paxman: Is it full of bores?

(Paxman asks himself the same question fourteen times)

Paxman: Well, since you are clearly not going to answer, why don't you just resign?

Paxman: Thank you very much, Jeremy. (*Paxman picks up newspapers and shuffles through them.*) Now, a quick look at tomorrow's papers. There's a piece here about Jeremy Paxman and Newsnight, another one here about Paxman at 50, a number of papers are carrying the Paxman story and the Sun here leads with the headline "Time To Pax It In Man"... Very amusing...

(Continued for the next 20 years)

A Taxi-Driver writes

Every week a well-known taxi driver writes on an issue of topical importance.

This week: 'The Afghan Hijack Drama' by **Jack "Boots" Straw** (Cab 4713)

BLIMEY, guv. See those Afghans, with their turbans and their funny beards? Comin' over here for a free handout from the social? Being put up at the bloody Hilton, excuse my French! What a bloody cheek! Pretending to be just a bunch of bona-fide hijackers, excuse my Latin! And they turn out to be a bunch of scroungers! Know what I'd do with them? Cut their hands off and pack 'em off home! I 'ad that General Pinochet in the back of the cab once. Lovely gentleman. Gave me a good tip. "Any trouble," he said, "shoot 'em." Very clever man!

NEXT WEEK: Annie Widdecombe (Cab No. 999) on 'Why they should string up these Afghan asylum-seekers and cut off their testicles.'

That Pinochet Medical Report In Full

94 HARLEY ST
LONDON W1

Highly Secret And Confidential

Re: General Pinochet

Dear Home Secretary,

In accordance with your wishes, I have examined the above patient and find him to be suffering from the following serious conditions:

1. The general is very elderly and hard of hearing. When I asked him a simple question, "Did you murder all those people?" he did not hear a word I said and continued to stare out of the window. This is what we doctors call defectio auralensis normalis.

2. The general's eyesight is also degenerating fast. When shown pictures of people he had murdered, he said he could not see them. This was clear evidence of what we doctors call ocularis degenerationis normalis.

3. The general's power of memory is virtually nil. Asked to recall the events of his dictatorship and his part in the deaths of thousands of people, he stared at me for a long time and asked whether Mrs Thatcher was coming to tea. This is a definite sign of what we call insanitatio fascistici normalis.

On all these grounds, it is the general's conclusion that he is unfit to stand trial and wishes to be returned home to Chile as soon as possible. I have every confidence that this will meet with your approval.

Signed,

Dr Emmanuel Straw (no relation)
F.R.L.E. J.V.S. C.D.Sc.

PS. I have pleasure in enclosing my bill for 25,000 guineas (cash, please!)

PINOCHET LATEST HEALTH SHOCK

> I'm so senile I've forgotten that I can't walk

Lines Written On The 50th Anniversary Of Sir Edward Heath's Entry Into The House Of Commons

by **William Rees-McGonagall**

*It was in the year nineteen hundred and fifty
When young Edward Heath was thinner and more nifty
That he first took his seat on the Tory backbenches
And unlike his colleagues had no eye for the wenches.*

*When he arrived they all said, "Ted's a bit of a bore,
But the fact is, old boy, he had a bloody good war.
And although he talks in an odd-sounding voice,
For the job of Chief Whip he's the obvious choice."*

*Then in the year nineteen hundred and sixty-two
Mr Macmillan said, "I've got an even more
                        important job for you to do.
We've got to join this Common Market show
So off to Brussels with your Belgian
                        phrasebook you must go."*

*Mr Heath did his utmost his leader to please
By negotiating a special rate for such foodstuffs
                        as Commonwealth cheese.
So Britain to her neighbours was brought even closer
And for his pains Mr Heath was soon
                        christened "The Grocer".*

*Then when the Tories got rid of Sir A. Douglas-Home
They decided it was time for a classless new broom.
"We cannot have another Old Etonian gent,
We'd better try this common little oik from Kent."*

*And so it was that after five years then
The Grocer arrived in triumph at "Number Ten".
But, alas, he was not intended to stay there for long
After his 3-day week went so disastrously wrong.*

*And all too soon it was curtains for Ted
When the Tory Party chose Mrs Thatcher instead.
Edward moved to the backbenches his increasing bulk
Where he embarked on the world's longest-ever sulk.*

*For 30 years he sat there and glowered
At the woman the Tories had so cruelly empowered.
Not since the noble Achilles retired to his tent
Had there been such a sulker as the Grocer from Kent.*

*And so in his 50th parliamentary year
He came to look back over his long and glorious career.
What had he achieved, this octogenarian bachelor?
Only to be annoyed by "that woman",*
                        Mrs Margaret Thatchler.

This tribute in verse was commissioned and paid for by the Anglo-Chinese Poetry and Trade Society, in association with the Rev. Sun K. Moon, Universal Church of Money Inc. of Seoul.

THE HUMAN BODY

Episode 94 THE SPINE

(Jolly music as Doctor with amusing moustache appears)

Professor Lord Winston *(for it is he)*: Now there is nothing more vital to the human being than the backbone.

(Winston walks into X-Ray machine)

Take a look at mine. See, I haven't got one. Which leads to real problems. For instance, I have great difficulty standing up.

(Winston walks into Alastair Campbell and collapses onto floor like lump of jelly)

Without any backbone I've lost my nerve. And this affects other parts of the body as well. Like my mouth.

(Giant close-up of Winston's mouth)

I say things about the health service and then I get a bit scared and deny them.

(Close-up of Professor Winston's bottom)

And I never said that either.

(Cut back to Winston lying on floor)

Next week I'll be looking at the arm and how easily it can be twisted. Aaargh!

(Man with moustache is given kicking by computer-generated hologram of the Prime Minister. More jolly music)

Ends

"Henry, will you please stop swatting flies with mother?"

WOODHEAD ATTACKS REMOVAL OF CLAUSE 28

by Our Education Correspondent **Lolita May**

THE CHIEF Inspector of Schools Chris Woodhead has insisted that Clause 28 must be retained to stop pupils being instructed in dubious sexual practices.

"Just consider the shocking case of one 16-year-old girl," he told reporters, "who was taught that a squalid sexual liaison with a second-rate thirty-something teacher had the same moral equivalence as that of two consenting homosexual adults entering into a committed long-term relationship."

"It turns my stomach," agreed his ex-wife.

Mr Woodhead is 24 (years older than her).

THE TEMPORA

MM A.D.

Solus X Dinarii Hodie!

Caesar Gives Top Job To Brutus

by Our Political Staff **W.F. Ides**

Londinium, Friday
IN A bold reshuffle of his Cabinet, Caesar today appointed Brutus to one of the key positions in his forum team.

Hague Caesar!

Brutus, who was rumoured at one point to be challenging Caesar for the leadership, has made an astonishing comeback and yesterday pledged his full loyalty to Caesar.

"I am totally behind Julius," he said. "Wherever he goes I'll be lurking around behind him."

Et tu Brutillo?

His recall comes after Caesar has been concerned about his loss of popularity and the lack of a "big-hitter" amongst his close associates.

"Brutus's role is to go on the attack," said Caesar. "I really want him to put the knife in."

HAT WEARS EMBARRASSING ROYAL

by Our Court Correspondent
Edward Furcoat-Amory

ONLOOKERS gasped in amazement yesterday when a respectable fur hat was seen out with a controversial blonde PR woman.

Last night the world of fur was outraged. "This is very embarrassing. What sort of message does it send out?" said top furrier Cruella de Vil.

WESSEX APPEAL

The fur hat later apologised, saying it had no idea that the Royal was real. "I thought she was a fake," it told reporters reporters.

(Reuters)

CHANNEL FOUR IN PORN STORM

by Our Media Staff **Phil Airtime**

SWITCHBOARDS at Channel Four were jammed last night as millions of angry viewers rang to complain about the broadcasting of a programme which did not feature a history of the clitoris, a discussion of vibrators or an exposé of the porn industry in eastern Europe.

Said one furious viewer, "I was sitting there on the couch waiting for something good and raunchy to come up, when the titles appeared for a programme called *Cold Tits*.

"I thought, this'll be a bit of alright, possibly featuring steamy love romps in the igloo by members of the Inuit community.

"But imagine my shock and disgust to see instead a load of old blokes walking about in a German castle and talking about making a glider during the war.

"How dare Channel Four pump stuff like this into my living room without warning! In future, I shall only watch Channel Five, a station where they understand that we want non-stop, round-the-clock soft porn without interruption."

David Elstein is 69.

BORES 28

Storm Grows

by Our Political Staff
Charles Boore

THE BIGGEST political row to have rocked Westminster for generations today exploded onto the front pages of every newspaper in the country.

"Could this be the hot potato that is going to bring down the Blair government?" asked hundreds of columnists. "Or is it the final nail in the Tories' coffin?"

The issue is simple. Should the infamous "Bores 28" stay or go?

And what is "Bores 28"? It is the law which makes it illegal to promote being a bore as being an equally acceptable life-style to talking about something interesting.

Said one anti-Bores 28 campaigner, "It is outrageous to discriminate against people simply on the grounds that they are boring.

"It is a basic human right to go on about unimportant issues rather than things that really matter."

Meanwhile, a pro-Bores 28 activist said, "It is outrageous that young people are being taught that it is perfectly OK to go around being boring at an early age."

ON OTHER PAGES

Millions of pieces about Bores 28 by the **Archbishop of Canterbury**, **Peter Tatchell**, **Cardinal Winning**, **Simon Heffer**, **Suzanne Moore** etc etc.

YESTERDAY

We don't
want to promote
homosexuality

TODAY

Congratulations!
You're promoted!

"Stop whingeing... I think it's nice when a husband and wife can work together"

RACE 'A FIX' CLAIMS HARE

by Our Man At The Finishing Post **E. Sopp**

ACCUSATIONS were flying last night when Dobbo the Tortoise was acclaimed as outright winner of the Mayoral Race.

Red Ken Hare, who had led from the beginning and crossed the line first, was amazed when the judges proclaimed Dobbo the winner.

The slow-moving Dobbo, it emerged, had been a last-minute choice after it became clear that the hare would win.

BLAIR & THE TORTOISE

"I only agreed to run," he said, "or, in my case, crawl very slowly, after the organiser Mr Blair assured me that I was bound to win, even if I lost."

Frank Dobson is 71.

SHOULD DOBBO SHAVE IT OFF?

YOU DECIDE

BEFORE

AFTER

It's the question every journalist is writing about. Now it's time for you, the public, to tell Dobbo what you think. Should he or shouldn't he?

To beard, or not to beard. That is the question.

Give us your "Frank" answer and help us fill up some more space.

Ring the Sun Beardline Now

YES ☎ 0800 24713   **YES** ☎ 0800 24714

TOMORROW: ● Should Tony Blair get rid of his silly grin? ● Should scrounging foreigners like Rupert Murdoch be sent home? (Shurely shome mistake?)

"Therefore, let us embrace the new technology with enthusiasm…"

Late News

SPECTATOR DEMANDS IMMEDIATE GUARDIAN 'DECOMMISSIONING'

by Our N. Ireland Correspondent

TROUBLE between the traditionally hostile Spectator and Guardian communities has broken out once again after the Guardian refused the Spectator's demands to "decommission its pro-IRA views".

The Guardian in turn accused the Spectator of being "nothing more than the Parajournalistic wing of the extreme Unionists".

Observers hoped that talks between Gerry Rusbridger and Boris Trimble might lead to a negotiated settlement, but negotiations faltered amidst vicious recriminations about *(continued over 94 pages)*

THE I.R.A   THE CONTINUITY I.R.A

THE REAL IRA   I CAN'T BELIEVE IT'S NOT THE I.R.A

SALLY JOCKSTRAP

ISN'T it pathetic that the entire country's sports writers have been reduced to commenting on a footballer's haircut? Is that all we have to say? Personally I think Becks has done the right thing because his earlier haircut made him seem effeminate with its blond highlighting and lank look, whereas the new close-crop adds immeasurably to his machismo and *(continued for 94 pages)*

Exclusive to all newspapers

YOUNG MAN HAS HAIRCUT

by Our Football Staff

ON OTHER PAGES

● Old man finds blonde girlfriend **2** ● Fat woman loses weight **3** ● Mozambique: millions dead **94**

I've got nothing up top

'BLOODY PAYDAY' INQUIRY BEGINS

by Our Nothern Ireland Staff **London Derry Irvine**

THERE WERE shock scenes in Derry yesterday as a vast army of lawyers marched through the streets to the town hall demanding their right to receive fees for two years' work on an inquiry.

Said the leader of Lawyers For Money (LFM), Sir Charles Hugefee QC: "For too long we lawyers have not been given any money for the shocking events of 1972. It is time that we had redress for this appalling abuse of our rights."

The lawyers then barricaded the town hall, erecting a huge wall of laptop computers, bundles of affidavits and irrelevant documents costing a lot of money, as they chanted *We Shall Overcharge*, their favourite protest song.

BLOODY SUNDAY TELEGRAPH

"We don't care how long it takes," said Mr Michael Cashcard QC, "nor do we care what the findings of the inquiry will be. The important thing is that, at the end of the day, we unearth a vast pile of public money in our bank accounts."

The cost of the inquiry is estimated at £2 billion.

"Tell you what... banks aren't as popular as they used to be"

POLICE WANT 'CRIME TO BE LEGALISED'

by Our Drugs Staff **Lynda Lee-Potsmoker**

A SPOKESMAN for the Police Federation last night argued that it was time to legalise crime in Britain. Said Inspector "Crackhead of the Yard" Cracker, "Let's be honest. Trying to catch criminals is wasting a lot of police time which could be better spent harassing motorists."

He continued, "Legalising crime would be a logical solution to the problem. If we simply de-criminalised crime then no one would be breaking the law and we would have reversed the rising crime rate at a stroke.

"A lot of young people," he concluded, "are attracted to crime merely because it is illegal. If it was legal to break the law then obviously you would find no criminals on the street.

"Wow!" he added. "Have you got any more of that stuff?"

DAILY TELEGRAPH

Letters to the Editor

Mr. Mandelson's interview on Irish radio

SIR — Millions of acting and former servicemen all over the world will have been outraged and appalled by Mr. Peter Tatchell's description of the Household Division as "chinless wonders". Mr. Mandelstam is too young and, dare one say it, too effeminate, to have served in any capacity in Her Majesty's armed forces. Furthermore, it is clear to me, and to all other unbiased observers, that he is a screaming nancy boy of the first order and unfit to hold office, even in what that great man President Mugabe (in my day British Rumbabaland) so rightly described as Mr. Blair's "Cabinet of gays".

> MAJ. GEN. SIR HORACE CHINDIT-WONDER
> The Last Posthouse,
> Aldershot, Hants

Mr Mandelson
An Apology

The Household Division of the British Army would like to apologise for their remarks last week suggesting members of the Labour Government were "brainless wonders". Their description of people like Mr Mandelson "strutting around in silly suits drinking pink champagne at pointless ceremonies" was unfortunate.

They now accept that Mr Mandelson is not "a brainless wonder" but a very brave politician doing a difficult job sucking up to an Irish audience on an obscure radio show.

GLENDA SLAGG

SIR PAUL McCARTNEY!?! Doesn't your heart go out to him as he tells us that he's found true love again!! And the lovely late Linda, speaking from heaven, has given her blessing on the union between the Rock legend and his limbless lovely?!! Forgive me if a tear is falling on the page as I pen this tribute to Macca's Magic Indian Summer Of Love!!! And should she die as well, I can only pray that Sir Paul would soon find a new love to lighten his long and winding road!!

HATS OFF to Vanessa Feltz — or Sveltz as I'm now going to call her (geddit?!?!). Only yesterday she was the size of an elephant, and now you can hardly see her if she stands sidways!!?!? She's given hope to millions of fatties all over the world!?!?! And how did she turn from Hatti Jacques to Posh Spice!?!?! Who cares?!!!?

VANESSA FELTZ — who do you think you are trying to kid??! Vanessa Fatz more like!!?!

Admit it, darling, you're just as vast as ever, give or take a few tons!!?!

Slimline!?!? Dream on!!! You still make Dawn French look like Twiggy!?!?!

HERE they are — Glenda's Halloween Love Pumpkins! (Geddit??)

● **GEOFFREY ROBINSON**!?! I've got some dirty pictures I could show you, Mr New Statesman!?!

● **MICHAEL DOUGLAS**!!?! OK, so you're very, very old, but can we get married, so I can divorce you for $45 million?? Pleazzze!!?!!

● **THE ENTIRE NEW ZEALAND PACK**!? Mmmm!? Scrum-ptious?!?! Geddit!!! Go on, let me have a try!!?!

Byeeee!?!

BRITAIN'S 100 YOUNGEST BORES

Who are they, the whizz-kid high-flyers who are toppling the older-established bores off their perch? They're young, they're dynamic, and they're incredibly boring.

Martha Lame-Duck, 21, who started lose-money.dot.con 6 months ago in her Stoke Poges bedroom, and is  today worth an estimated £10.2 billion. Says Martha, "I suppose I am very boring, but it's not being boring that's important. It's the challenge and the excitement of being at the cutting edge of the new Millennium."

Julian Anorak, 17, who started caffe-latte.dot.con selling on-line coffee to mobile phone users from his parents' Worplesdon  garage only three months ago, is now worth an estimated £179.5 billion. Says Julian: "OK, so I'm incredibly boring. But being boring's not what turns me on. I just happen to believe in cyber-latte, OK?"

Vikram Sixpak, 19, who launched poppa.dom.cot, Britain's first internet-based poppadom retailing operation, from the top of a No. 19 bus,  and is today worth an estimated £1,821 billion. Says Vikram: "Being boring is a very small part of the pleasure I get from my company. The main thing is to be at the interface of vertically-integrated pappadum delivery and the growing needs of e-customers in a global economy." *(That's enough e-bores. Ed.)*

"Are we there yet, Dad?"

SEARCH

Nursery Times

FRIDAY MARCH 24 2000

Market Goes Wild Over New Internet Flotation

by Our Fairy-tale Staff **Mother Lane Goose**

THERE were scenes of frenzied buying in the Stock Exchange today as shares in the new internet sensation emperorsnewclothes.com went on the market.

The company which provides an online retail quality garment service for members of the Imperial family was estimated to be worth a staggering 100 billion sovereigns.

However, a little boy analyst was worried that the company has so far provided very little in the way of visible results. "This is just naked greed. There's just nothing there."

But supporters are unworried.

Said a Mr Humpty Dumpty, "I've put all my savings into emperorsnew-clothes.com and I'm

absolutely confident in their prospects. You certainly won't find me jumping off the top of a high wall when it all goes wrong."

HOW I DISCOVERED ✝ TRUE ✝ PENITENCE

by Sir Jonathan of Aitken

Exclusive to the Sunday Times (Because No One Else Would Spend £150,000 On Such Garbage)

SINCE my imprisonment I have come to terms with my past. I have had to face up to the fact that I did wrong in the sight of God. The crime I committed was a minor slip which anyone could have made, and which in fact was not a crime at all. It was only because the media were jealous that I went to Eton and Oxford, and was very good-looking, and was very rich with lots of houses and beautiful girlfriends, that I went to gaol at all. But now I have paid the price for my sins. Not that they were sins. I was just unlucky and a Conservative at the wrong time. But I forgive all those who persecuted me, the bastards.

Next week: I Know Where You Live Rusbridger – And So Do My Mates From D Wing!

© World Copyright Sunday Crimes.

NEW-LOOK QUEEN

Lucky lavender, dear?

ZIMBABWE BROADCASTING CORPORATION

Radio Highlights

2.00pm The Archers
Nigel and Elizabeth weigh up the cost of new furnishings for Lower Loxley. Pat and Helen plan the perfect lemon curd preserve for the school fete. Meanwhile, at Grange Farm, Shula and David are being dragged from their beds by a group of marauding tribesmen who beat them both to within an inch of their life with sharpened sticks before seizing the farm.

STEPHEN LAWRENCE
Amazing New Breakthrough

by Our Crime Staff **Roger Crook**

IN A stunning development in the Stephen Lawrence case, Inspector Knacker of the Yard today revealed that he may have found the murder weapon.

"We have searched high and low for this," he told reporters, "and I have even sent men to the West Indies to follow up possible leads.

"But recently we had a major new tip-off when someone rang up and said 'Have you thought of looking in the garden of the chief suspect Mr Adolf Yobbo?'

"As it turned out this was a significant development and, sure enough, after only seven years we found the knife right there in the garden.

"This is police work of the highest order," he concluded. "And we should be making arrests any century now."

The Daily Telegraph

The Advantages of Legalisation

IT is now time to think the unthinkable and admit for the first time that attempts to control the sale of the Daily Telegraph have been an abject failure. It is freely available on most high streets, railway stations and supermarkets and it is estimated that over a million people "take" the Daily Telegraph regardless of the damage it can do to their health.

And let us not underestimate the side effects. Medical research has proved that regular consumption of the Telegraph leads to degeneration of the mental faculties. Readers become alternatively depressed and disgusted, particularly if they live in Tunbridge Wells. Some imagine that they see the first cuckoo of spring in March and others become paranoid, suffering from the delusion that millions of asylum-seekers are swarming into their bedrooms and stealing their womenfolk.

But there are positives. People who are old or incurably insane can benefit from "doing" the crossword on a regular basis.

Surely Jack Straw must be bold enough to recognise that the Daily Telegraph is a fact of life whether we like it or not.

Keeping it underground only helps the fortunes of peddlars, dealers and unsavoury barons from Canada.

Should we not decriminalise the Daily Telegraph now? Let us know what you think by ringing our new Dopeline or e-mailing us at www.pot.com

© *Charles Moorijuana, The Old Spliffery, Cannabis Square.*

Shock News in Brief

Middle-aged English women keep their clothes on **2**
John Thaw not in ITV drama **3**
Exclusive: no interview with Ali G **4**
Interesting article in Spectator **94**

POLLY FILLER

MESSAGE to fellow female columnists: Please, please, spare us the gory details of your pregnancies!

Just because Cherie Blair and Iman are mothers-to-be, it doesn't mean we all want to read endless pieces by women journalists about how God-awful their morning sickness is, and how scatty they've become, and how useless and unsympathetic their partners are!

We've all been there, done that and got the blood-stained T-shirt! Come on, girls, surely pregnancy is too intimate and private an experience just to use as copy fodder for lazy hackettes who want to write from home?

It would be all too easy for me to tell readers about how Simon carried on playing five-a-side with his mates from the on-line section while my waters broke; or how, when expecting Charlie, I once felt so sick at a press conference I vomited into the fashion editor's Gucci handbag; or how my brain became so mushy during pregnancy that I put the pizza in the washing machine and my knickers in the microwave! And, as for haemorrhoids and stretch marks, I could tell you a few tales – and I've still got the rubber ring. *(Please stop. Ed.)*

But I'm not going to waste your time pretending that my experience is somehow topical. What's it got to do with Cherie Blair or Iman that I got weepy in the afternoons and watched Bambi ten times on video? Or had cravings for Firelighter and Peanut Butter sandwiches?

Everyone's pregnancy is special to them, and I personally think that the birth of Charlie enriched my life beyond measure, but I don't go around telling everyone about it!

No, my only advice to Cherie and Iman is to make sure that Tony and David pull their weight, help out with the housework and don't slope off to the Sports Bar with the widescreen to watch women's kick-boxing from Thailand – like some partners I could mention, ie the Useless Simon. And my advice to my desperate colleagues in print is find a new subject to write about for all of our sakes!

Next Week: Polly Filler Is Pregnant.

55

QUESTION TIME BIAS
BBC Attacked

by Our Media Correspondent **Phil Space**

THE Prime Minister has issued a formal complaint alleging bias in TV's popular "Question Time – Live From The House Of Commons".

"Every week," says the complaint, "the Tory leader William Hague is allowed to appear and get the better of me.

"The Speaker fails to intervene and the viewer is left with the impression that I am a fool with nothing to say about the issues of the day.

"I demand that Mr Hague is replaced in future programmes in the interests of political balance and fair play. A suitable replacement might be Sooty or perhaps the late John Major."

"O.K! I admit it. You're a Renaissance man"

PRAVDARIEL

BIRTISM SWEPT AWAY AS DYKOV UNVEILS FIVE YEAR PLAN

by Our BBC Staff **Raymond Snodoff**

THERE were scenes of jubilation in the streets of White City (formerly Birtograd) as delighted workers began pulling down statues of the hated dictator John Birt and smashing the symbols of his Birtist regime.

Already thousands of apparatchiks appointed by Birt have been removed from office by the new leader whose five year plan has been interpreted as an attempt to repair the damage done by Birt's "non-cultural revolution".

Red Square Eyes

Birt has been airbrushed from all official BBC pictures and declared a non-person.

Schoolchildren will be taught that the Director Generalship of the BBC was passed directly from Michael Checklandov, the architect of the accountancy revolution, to the much-loved Greg Dykov or "Roland Ratski" as he is affectionately known by his comrades.

Announcing his plans to a cheering meeting of loyalists (Alan Yentoff, Mark Thomsonovitch and Jenny Abramski), the leader looked forward to a new golden era.

"Comrades," he said, "my five year programme is simple. It will be a repeat of all our current programmes for the next five years."

● *There will be another chance to see Comrade Dykov's speech at 3.00am on BBC Choice.*

Stop Press

John Birt is believed to be in an asylum for the insane somewhere in Westminster under the assumed name of Baron Birt.

Dr Thomas Stuttaford

CANCER can affect people in many different ways. To some it may seem a debilitating and possibly fatal illness, but to the dynamic individual aged 69 or so there is little likelihood that it will cause any lasting ill-effects. It may even be beneficial, leading to increased dynamism and virility, particularly if the individual concerned has recently married a younger oriental partner and has expanded his business activities in the Far East. Such a person will probably live to be a hundred and may never die, according to recent research at the Stuttaford Clinic of Sycophantic Medicine.

© *A. Doctor.*

LATE NEWS

CANCER FOUND TO HAVE 'MURDOCH'

DOCTORS confirmed last night that a well-known cancer has contracted Rupert Murdoch but insisted that the Murdoch could be successfully removed with no harmful effects. Said a specialist, "Obviously it sounds frightening to be told you have the big M, but with today's treatments it is no longer terminal." *(Reuters)*

The Editor Of The Sunday Telegraph Dominic Lawson Gives An Exclusive Interview To The Daily Telegraph

by Our Media Staff **Terry Graph**

THERE is no more prestigious prize in world journalism than the Tobacconist And Retailers Gazette Newspaper Of The Year Award.

So no wonder that this year it was the turn of the Sunday Telegraph to win it.

I had the privilege of interviewing the paper's much-loved editor Dominic Lawson, who graciously gave me five minutes of his time while he was working out how to put the words "Newspaper of the Millennium" all over the front page.

"Some people say, Sir Dominic, that you are a little aggressive on occasions. Is that true?"

"Who said that?" he snarled in reply. "Their days are numbered, whoever they are. I'll track them down. Just you see if I don't! Now get out, you bastard!"

I left him to his difficult job which he performs with such astonishing skill.

© *InterTelegraph Promotions.*

"How do you put this child-lock on the internet?"

LEGAL SYSTEM COULD BREAK DOWN UNDER WEIGHT OF MONEY, IRVINE WARNS

by Our Legal Staff **Joshua Rosenbeard**

THE Lord Chancellor last night painted a horrifying picture of the collapse of Britain's judicial system as lawyers are forced to take on millions of new cases under the new EU Human Rights Act, due to come into force next autumn.

Said Lord Irvine, "We have not enough courts in the country to accommodate all the money which this Act is going to pour into our coffers."

DERRY RICH

"It is appalling," said the Lord Chancellor. "You have no idea just how much we lawyers will make from these ridiculous cases.

"I know of one lady lawyer," he went on, "with a husband, four children and a large house in Downing Street to support, who stands to hit the jackpot as a result of this ridiculous new law being put on the statute book by her husband."

ON OTHER PAGES
Who Wants To Be A Millionblair?

Your chance to join the gravy train of the future!!!

Simply complete the following sentence:

"I would like to join Matrix Chambers so that I can fight for the rights of the underprivileged and make a great deal of ..."

"This is it? The four-poster bed?"

A Taxi Driver writes

Every week a well-known cab driver is asked to write about an issue of topical importance. This week:

Mickey Caine (Cab No. 3294) on attitudes to success.

IT's a bloody liberty guv'nor the way they treat achievers in this country, guv, I mean everyone hates you if you're successful over here, all they do is give you money and awards and all that but if you don't talk proper you'll always be an outsider, no, this country's finished, if I had my way I'd go and live in the States where it isn't a crime to be famous and to make a few million quid by sheer bloody graft no them people at Bafta should be strung up – it's the only language they understand... BAFTA you know what it stands for guv? Bastards And Fat Toffee Nosed Arseholes... Ha ha ha ha I 'ad that Lord Olivier in the back of the cab once very nice gentleman, lovely way of talking, I could have listened to him all night...

*NEXT WEEK: **Tony Hopkins** (Welsh Cab No. 7324): Why I reckon Britain is finished as well.*

STEPHEN NORRIS'S BIG DAY

I say, look at that bridesmaid!

ENGLAND CAPTAIN TOOK CATCH

by Our Entire Cricket Staff **Christopher Simon-Jenkins of Hillhead**

THE world of cricket was rocked to its foundations yesterday by the shock revelation that the captain of the England cricket team had "taken a catch" in order to change the results of a match.

The controversy, which threatens to end the game of cricket as we know it, centres on a triangular series between England, Rumbabwe (formerly British Rumbabaland) and the Gilbert and Sullivan Islands.

AMAZING W.G. GRACE

Police watching the game were startled to see the ball travelling at speed towards an England fielder who, rather than running out of the way, stood his ground and held it in his hands for long enough for the Rumbabwean batsman to be given out.

"Our suspicions were immediately aroused by this uncharacteristic action," said Inspector Knackerjee of the Gujarat Crime Squad, "and our enquiries have led us to the conclusion that the England captain was deliberately trying to confound the punters by 'swinging the game' England's way."

Late News

England Captain "Threw" Ball
(Reuters)

OWMUCHIZZAT?!

Cricket Scandal

Have You Found Salvation?

asks **L. Ron Aitken,** Chief Minister of the Church of Lientology

SINNERS! You too can experience the joys of repentance and forgiveness through the wise words of L. Ronathan Aitken:

"Brothers and sisters! I confess before Almighty God that I too once did wrong – but not really. And I was made to pay the price.

Now I am asking you to pay the price too. Only £99.99, from the Daily Telegraph Book Club. *(Surely "Crook Blub"? Ed.)* Send now for your copy of my personal testament 'I Am The Way, The Truth and The Lie' by L. Ron Aitken."

Some testimony from fellow Lientologists

N. Hamilton writes: *"Like L. Ron I was innocent and the media crucified me. But since I discovered L. Ron's path to money and being on television, I am once again happy."*

J. Archer writes: *"Like L. Ron I did nothing wrong and the media ruined my life. All I did was tell a few lies. But now thanks to the Church of Lientology, I realise I was telling the truth all along."*

Now, you too can walk with your head held high, thanks to the greatest relgous teacher since the Rev. Sun K. Moon.

Daily Mail, Friday, April 7, 2000

Good Riddance To An Evil Monster

by **Dr Theodore Dullpimple** of The Spectator

Disgusting

I SAY this. When the history of the 20th Century comes to be written, the evils of Stalin and Hitler will pale into insignificance compared with the moral chaos unleashed by a small man with a pipe sitting in Cambridge.

His name – Dr Alex Comfort, author of the notorious Joy Of Sex manual which did more damage to Western civilisation than Mein Kampf and Mao's Little Red Book put together.

The permissive society, unleashed by Comfort's evil notion that sex is somehow enjoyable, has brought a tidal wave of misery, and human suffering, in terms of broken homes, abortions, teenage pregnancies, child abuse and articles by Polly Toynbee in the Guardian.

Keep On Going, This Is Better Than Paul Johnson

Make no mistake. The world is well rid of this seedy little doctor with his boring articles in the Spectator about how ghastly the working classes are, particularly when they take their trousers off.

© *Dr A. Daniels, Mailtrash Productions, in association with the Spectacularlyboring.*

"It was my Joanne's last wish... that I invite our dearest friends round and eat her"

TEBBIT'S EMPLOYMENT POLICY REVISITED I

On yer website!

TEBBIT'S EMPLOYMENT POLICY REVISITED II

On yer mobile!

JAY PEERAGE STINKS says Ashcroft

by Our House of Lords Staff **Lord Conrad Black Rod**

IN A stinging attack on the leader of the House of Lords, Lord Ashcroft of Selize described Baroness Jay's peerage as "a scandal that stinks to high heaven".

"This woman," he said, "has only been given a title because her father was the Prime Minister and she sucked up to Tony Blair. I had to pay good money for my peerage and this woman has got one for free.

"It is an outrage," he continued.

"What sort of democracy is this? Surely anyone with enough money should be entitled to buy their way into the upper chamber?"

In another unpleasant outburst Sir Edward Heath in turn attacked Lord Ashcroft.

"This man has made a fortune from a dodgy third world country," said Sir Edward, 96, "whereas I have received huge cheques from the Chinese, particularly their delightful premier Mo Dem Down, who was unjustly accused of massacring..." *(cont. p.94)*

Guerilla Gardeners' Question Time

with Anna Kist

Caller: When is the best time of year to plant a brick through the windows of McDonalds?

Anna: Any time of the year is good, but spring is traditional. Make sure you've got a nice big brick and make a great big hole in the window. With any luck, in 6 months' time you'll see a lovely "For Sale" notice where the shop was.

Caller: Hello Anna, can you recommend the best seeds of destruction for world capitalism and the international finance system?

Anna: I suggest you grow a nice green mohican or maybe a red beard. Then strip off all your clothes and behave as if you're in the nursery. This should do the trick.

Caller: How can I help to provide more green spaces in London?

Anna: The best thing to do is to find a nice grassy area with plenty of flowers like Parliament Square and then dig it all up and put it on the road for the dustmen to throw away.

Caller: Hello, Anna, it's Tony Benn from the Flowerpot Men. Have you got any cure for madness caused by drinking too much tea?

Anna: Well, you should...

Benn: I'm not listening to you because you're part of the ruling capitalist media, but I am recording this conversation because I know you will distort my views...

CLASS WAR HERO

This was their finest hour

THE ALTERNATIVE VOICE

Dave Spart, Senior Co-Ordinator Of The Neasden Anarchists Against Burgers Collective

ONCE again, the capitalist media have cynically over-reacted in typical knee-jerk fashion to the totally and utterly peaceful violent demonstrations against international capitalism er... on May Day the so-called defacing of the Churchill statue was typically misrepresented by the right-wing press since it was actually a totally legitimate act of protest against a fascist warmonger who cold-bloodedly fought against Hitler who was er... a vegetarian who totally opposed fox-hunting and even organised demonstrations against international capitalism according to respected historian David Irving er... *(Cont'd. p. 94)*

Exclusive To All Newspapers

HAVE YOU SEEN THESE THUGS?

Do you know the identities of these mindless hooligans – responsible for defacing countless statues and war memorials in London?

If you recognise any of these pigeons phone Scotland Yard or the tabloid paper of your choice today.

ANARCHIST CO-ORDINATOR IDENTIFIED

Let's take over the capital

PLAYGROUND

Anthony Powell's Journal
March 2000

Tuesday 28 March

WOKE UP to find myself dead, on reflection a not wholly disagreeable state. In fact a certain status conferred: Shakespeare, Kipling, Stendahl, others one could think of, all passed through what must be admitted a disconcerting process. Absence of "essentials of life" – Debrett, *Daily Telegraph*, etc — obvious drawback, tho' not, one suspects, insuperable.

Wednesday 29 March

ARRIVAL in Heaven. Rather a business. A great crowd of supplicants, none of them known to me, finally disposed into some kind of order by arrival of imposing figure in flowing blue and white robes (the Hon. G.H. Lyttelton's house colours). This I took to be Archangel Gabriel, tho' no formal introduction. Elysian fields, glimpsed beyond gates, not unlike lower meadows at Eton. General impression – soaring pediments, arches etc – not at all unfavourable in point of view of architectural style, tho' could have done without interminable piped "sacred" music.

Thursday 30 March

DINNER for new arrivals. All perfectly tolerable. God — venerable figure, curiously like Andrew (Devonshire) — perfectly all right once one gets to know him, at pains to put guests at their ease with jokes about "fiery furnaces beneath" etc. Wine Ambrosia 2000 (I did not see the label). Conversation about war, pestilence, death etc – not subjects on which I am outstandingly hot – but was pleased to discover that attendant cherubim distant connexion of my mother's Lincolnshire Cherry-Bymme offshoots.

Friday 31 March

IRRITATED to find among accounts of other new arrivals in social column of Daily Heavenograph reference to "Lady Barbara Twytte" (widow of my Balliol contemporary Gavin Twytte). In fact, as merest glance at appropriate reference books could have shown — tho' possibly not procurable here — Barbara, as baronet's relict, merely "Lady Twytte". Naturally such sloppiness endemic "down below", as I shall no doubt have to get used to calling it, but somewhat shocked to find celestial standards similarly lax (*Continued page 94 of Book of Life*).

THE QUESTION THAT STUMPED TV CAROL

by Our Media Correspondent **Hugh Wantstobeamillionaire**

THE nation was gripped last night by a thrilling battle of wits between Britain's brainiest women – Carol Borderver and Kirsty Yawn.

The nail-biting competition to raise their profiles (*Surely "Money for Charity"? Ed.*) reached a sensational climax when host Chris Tarrantless asked Borderver: *What was top showbiz writer William Shakespeare's first name?*

Was it:

a) Cedric?

b) Kevin?

c) Gazza?

d) Peregrine Worsthorne?

ITV chiefs later admitted that their researchers had made the question too hard and it was no wonder that TV Carol had such problems with it.

The correct answer is of course "Macbeth".

Kirsty fared even worse and stumbled in the second round when asked: *Who are you?*

Are you:

a) Carol Smillie?

b) Kirsty Wark?

c) Mariella Frostrup?

d) Baroness Jay of Paddington?

Kirsty asked to ask the audience, 75% of whom said she was Charlie Dimmock (*Cont. p. 94*)

The Last Giant Of Letters Is Dead
by A.N. Wislon

PROUST. Shakespeare. Powell. The unbroken line of English literary genius has been broken at last by the tragic and untimely death at the age of 94 of A.N. Powell, with his unforgettable 28-volume roman à fleuve *Come Dancing*.

Who can forget his galaxy of such unforgettable characters as... er... the Tarkington-Barkingtons, Lavinia Starborgling, the enigmatic J.R. Hartley, and my own particular favourite, Lady Ann Widdecombe.

We all of us, I think, have a Widdepool in our lives. And it is the character of Winderpool which will live for ever, alongside such giants of literature as Falstaff, Mr Pickwick and Jonathan Aitken. (*Not cont'd age 94*)

Exclusive to all newspapers

'I'M NOT JUST MRS JONATHAN ROSS' SAYS MRS JONATHAN ROSS

by Our Showbiz Staff **Phil Space**

A WOMAN with red hair today told the world much more than it wanted to know about her relationship with a man who appears on television.

What's it like being dead from the neck up?

Letters to the Editor

The Martin Case

SIR – For centuries it has been a cherished tenet of English law that an Englishman's home is his castle and that he has an inalienable right to defend his property against unwarranted intrusion by any means available to him, not excluding the detonation of a low-yield nuclear device should that seem appropriate. In the immortal judgment of Lord Justice Denning (1402-1998) in the case of Farmer Giles v. the late Nosher Stibbs, "Whomsoever ye may be, be ye ever so high or ever so low, if ye durst break in and enter upon ye dwelling place of a sovereign subject of Her Majestie Ye Queene Elizabeth ye Firste, ye shall not be surprised if ye aforesaid householder shall blast thee to Kingdom Come, and may God have mercie upon your soul."

What could be clearer than that?

LT. COL. B. FROBISHER
Auberon St Waugh
Somerset.

SIR – Having lived in the depths of rural Norfolk for more than half a century, I can testify that we count ourselves fortunate if we see a policeman once in a lifetime. Sadly, one came to our house only last week and, so surprised was I by his sudden appearance, that I shot him, under the misapprehension that he was an intruder. This means our local force has been reducd to zero. When will the Government act to remedy this disgraceful situation?

REV. JOSIAH BLUNDERBUSS
Widdecombe St Ann
Norfolk.

SIR – Having lived in the depths of rural Somerset for more than 10 minutes, I have now been burgled 87 times. Is this a record?

MRS SARAH BIRDBATH
The Old Breakin
Wrigley Chewett, Som.

SIR – Whatever next? Are we going to be arrested in our own homes for reading the Daily Telegraph?

MR DAVE TWERP-SMYTHE
Via e-mail.

SIR – Am I the first person in this part of rural Buckinghamshire to hear the welcome sound of the first shotgun of spring?

SIR H. GUSSETT
The Old Shooting Range
St Engun, Cornwall.

TORIES: SELF-DEFENCE JUSTIFIED

by Our Political Correspondent **William Rees-Mugger**

THE leader of the opposition, Mr William Hague, today defended his call for new laws to protect those on the receiving end of unprovoked attacks.

"Everyone has the right to defend themselves by any means at their disposal," he told supporters. "If someone is picking on you because you are weak and hopeless then you are entitled to do *anything* to save yourself.

TWELVE YEAR OLD BORE

"This must include," he continued, "using any weapon that is at hand, including desperate speeches about law and order and frenzied assaults on asylum seekers."

Hague quoted the recent sad example of an eccentric Yorkshireman who had been left to live alone in a deserted old Conservative Party. He was subject to repeated attacks by a gang of habitual politicians who had given him a kicking and stolen all his policies.

"Surely," said Mr Hague, "this man had no option but to shoot himself in the foot? And surely it is grossly unfair for him to be blamed for his tragic actions?

"No," he concluded. "I am the victim here, not the dangerous criminal Tony Blair."

FRIDAY, MAY 5, 2000   NATIONAL NEWSPAPER OF THE YEAR

GUTLESS GERMAINE FAILS TO KILL INTRUDER

By Our Entire Staff

IN A tragedy which has stunned the entire nation, fenland recluse Dr Germaine Greer failed to murder a teenage intruder who had broken into her remote East Anglia farmhouse.

Greer, 61, regarded as "a bit of an oddball" by her Saffron Walden neighbours, lives alone in a ramshackle Georgian hideaway with only her geese for company.

Yet, when confronted with a clear opportunity to blast an unwelcome teenage visitor with both barrels of an illegal shotgun, she meekly allowed herself to be tied up and let her friends call the police to rescue her.

What sort of an example does this cowardly behaviour set to the nation's growing army of oddballs and recluses?

If we cannot rely on such people to take the law into their own hands, what sort of a Britain are we handing on to our children?

The Weird World of Batty Germaine

A LONE, unkempt figure in oily Wellington boots and a tattered old mac wanders over the fields scattering kitchen leftovers to an eager gaggle of hungry geese.

"Eat that, you bastards!" she shrieks in a gruff Australian accent.

She has become a hermit, shut off from the world behind the ivy-clad walls of her tumbledown retreat.

Occasionally, she is disturbed by malicious journalists disguised as homeless cripples, who abuse her hospitality and then mock her in the pages of the Daily Mail.

No wonder that (cont'd. p. 94)

POETRY CORNER

In Memoriam John Aspinall, gambler, zoo-keeper and Zulu chieftain

So. Farewell then
John Aspinall.
Amazingly you were not
Eaten by one of your
Tigers.

Keith's mum says
You will now be reunited
With your friend
Lord Lucan.

But Keith says he saw him
When he was on holiday
In Mozambique.

So you may have
To wait a while.

> E.J. "Thribbers" (17½)

In Memoriam Roger Vadim, French film-maker

So. Farewell then
Roger Vadim.
(Or should we say "Adieu"
Since you were
French?)

"Will you marry me?"
That was your
Catchphrase.

> Monsieur E.J. Thribb
> (dix-sept et demi)

Taken from E.J. Thribb's new award-winning translation of Beowulf *(Fabber & Fabber, £19.95)*

In Memoriam Gad Rausing, Swedish milk-carton tycoon

So. Farewell then
Gad Rausing.
Son of the man
Who invented
The cardboard
Milk carton.

"How are you supposed
To open this?"
That was your customers'
Catchphrase.

"I've got milk all
Over me."
That was another.

> E.J. Thribb (£17½ billion)

IT'S GRIM UP NORTH LONDON — KNIFE & PACKER

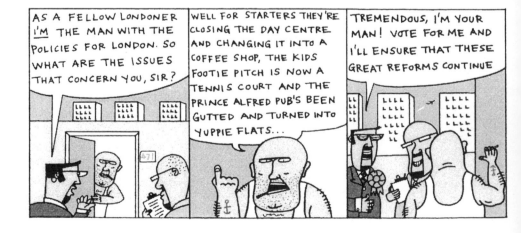

IT'S GRIM UP NORTH LONDON — KNIFE & PACKER

In Memoriam President Hafez Al-Assad of Syria

So. Farewell
Then
President Assad.

Ruthless Dictator
And Mass Murderer.

We are not As
Sad as the people
Who were crying on
The television.

Quite the opposite
In fact.

> E.J. Thribb (17½) whose new collection of political verse "Write and Left" is published on the internet.

Lines on the retirement of Michael Heseltine MP

So. Farewell
Then
Michael Heseltine,

Universally known
As Tarzan.

Except Tarzan
Was the King
Of the Jungle.

And the nearest
You got
Was Deputy King.

You never made
It to the
Top of the tree.

> Edgar Rice Thribb (17½)

In Memoriam David Tomlinson, Actor

So. Farewell
Then.
David Tomlinson.
Star of Mary
Poppins, Bedknobs and
Broomsticks and
Many other
Great films.

"Let's go fly
A kite up to
The Highest Height."
Yes, that was your
Catchphrase.

And
Where you
Are going
Now.

> E.J. Thribb (with lump in throat) 17½

Friday, May 19, 2000   30p   **THE PEOPLE'S PAPER**

DIGGER'S DAUGHTER DOES DIRTY ON DYING DAD

By Our Filth Staff **DAVID YELLOW**

BLONDE bombshell Liz Murdoch has not only dumped her hubbie! Now she's dumped her Dad as well!

The Dirty Digger's even-dirtier-daughter has shown her gratitude to her Sugar Daddy by giving him two fingers!

Randy Rupe gave lovely Liz a job at soaraway Sky TV, but when he didn't make her the Big Boss she thanked the suffering satellite supremo by blowing a big raspberry at him on his sickbed!

Said sorrowing Dad from his Peking Love Nest, "Elizabeth has shown no loyalty and treated me like dirt. She has behaved appallingly. I am proud to call her my daughter."

Sex-siren Liz meanwhile has got a bun in the oven courtesy of the King of the Spin, PR man Matthew Fraud, who is believed to be delighted with the news that his live-in partner Liz is up the duff. Said Matthew, in a quote that we have just made up in the office, "The baby will be a bastard — just like his grandfather." *(That's enough exaggerated, intrusive, half-baked tabloid drivel. Ed.)*

THE SON SAYS

Ha ha ha, I'm going to get it all! It's mine all mine!

© *L. Murdoch*

DANDO CASE —

14 MILLION NEW WITNESSES COME FORWARD

by Our Crime Staff **John Stalker**

POLICE investigating the year-old mystery of who shot TV presenter Jill Dando have been "inundated" with calls, following the latest BBC Crimewatch Special on the case.

Said a delighted Inspector "Knacker of the Yard" Knacker, "We've had over 14 million new witnesses coming forward, all of whom clearly recall seeing Miss Dando on television in the last week.

"We will be following up every one of these leads," said Inspector Knacker, "with the aid of 2500 officers drafted in from all over the country, particularly rural areas.

"If it takes 100 years and costs £1 billion," said the inspector, "it will all have been worth it.

"We have clearly narrowed down our search to someone of either sex, between the ages of 0 and 100, who has the psychological profile of a person who might wish to murder a TV personality.

"That is all I can say at this stage. Thank you, gentlemen. Was the tie alright?"

ON OTHER PAGES

Is Sporty Spice Too Fat?
Is Posh Spice Too Thin? **2**
Is Ginger Spice Too Old? **3**
Is Our Editor Too Thick? **4-94**

HITLER'S REPUTATION IN TATTERS

Holocaust 'inexcusable' says Judge

THE German war leader Adolf Hitler has had his reputation finally destroyed after a lengthy high court action.

In a two-hour judgement Mr Justice Cocklecarrot described the Führer as a "formerly respected statesman who has allowed himself to fall prey to right-wing obsessions and racist ideologies".

"His early work showed great promise," said the judge, "and he helped to create employment and build autobahns and Volkswagens. However, I have to conclude that Mr Hitler has ended up as a man with no respect for the truth who came to believe all the lies that David Irving told him."

After the hearing Mr Hitler said he would appeal.

"Oh no! Now I know I'm fat!"

HAGUE'S NEW BANDWAGON PLEDGE

by Our Political Staff Simon Hefferlump

MR William Hague, leader of the Conservative Party, today gave a firm promise that he would jump on any bandwagon that made itself available.

"For too long," he said in his peculiar voice, "we in the Tory Party have stood idly by and watched as a number of band-wagons have rolled past, with no attempt being made to jump on them at all."

THE HAGUE WAIN

"I give you my solemn pledge," Mr Hague continued, "that I will not hesitate to jump, as firmly as is necessary, on each and every new bandwagon that may appear now or at any time in the future."

Mr Hague is 17.

On other pages: ● Shoot Asylum Seekers, Says Hague ● Support Burglar Killers, Says Hague ● Jail Pokemon Bullies For Life, Says Hague ● Restore News At Ten Now, Says Hague ● Ban Rain On Bank Holidays, Says Hague.

MIRROR PRIDE OF BRITAIN AWARDS
A NATION WEEPS

by Mirror Editor Tears Morgan

Little Piers

Little Jason

THERE was not a dry eye in the land as the nation yesterday honoured the unsung heroes of Britain who have plucked the heartstrings of a whole *(Get on with it. Ed.)*

The top award went to little Piers Morgan who had bravely clung on to his own job while everyone around him was sacked. Little Piers showed amazing gall *(Surely 'courage'? Ed.)* as he refused to give in and selflessly let everyone else take the blame until he was finally rescued by his Chairman Sir Victor Blank.

TELEBLUBBIES

Choking back the tears, Sir Victor told an audience of weeping celebrities, "Piers is a symbol of Modern Britain. Greedy, shameless and ruthless. Today we salute him."

PRAT OF BRITAIN

The next award went to brave little Jason Fraser, the Mirror photographer who without a moment's hesitation took a picture of Camilla Parker Bowles in her swimsuit on a beach in Mauritius. Not stopping for a second to consider her privacy or his own shame and embarrassment little Jason displayed amazing pluck in selling the photographs for £100,000 to his co-winner, little Piers Morgan, who told him: "You have saved my circulation."

A weeping Michael Caine *(Cont. p. 94)*

Daily Mail
FRIDAY, APRIL 21, 2000   NATIONAL NEWSPAPER OF THE YEAR   35p

RED KEN: THE SHOCKING TRUTH

By Daily Mail Political Staff
Alasdair Campbell
(as told to Simon Heffer)

AT LAST the truth is out! Ken Livingstone, far from being just a cuddly TV personality and wise-cracking chat show guest, is in fact a politician.

Thousands of Ken supporters will be devastated when they realise that the warm-hearted newt-fancier from Harlesden is not the innocent celebrity that they had supposed, but a fully signed-up member of the political class, who has dedicated his entire life to gaining power and implementing his ideological agenda.

Have I Got Newts For You

The Mail can reveal the categorical proof of Ken's secret life behind the familiar playboy façade:

● Ken frequently makes unashamedly political speeches to curry favour with different groups of voters

● Ken makes promises which he has no intention of keeping

● Ken is prepared to say anything, however controversial, which he thinks will gain him publicity

● Ken will even consort with comedians, pop singers and other showbusiness personalities in an effort to seem like "a man of the people"

● Ken will happily accept "donations" from businessmen, the larger the better, to support his campaign to win power.

In all these respects, we can reveal, Ken Livingstone has shown that he is no different from Tony Blair.

How disillusioning that must be for his erstwhile supporters, who for so long were taken in by the cheeky chappie who pretended he was just "an ordinary bloke having a bit of a larf".

The Naked Witches

LONDON
The Most Exciting City In The World

THE unveiling of the new power station on the South Bank confirms London's position as the most exciting city in the world.

From every corner of the globe visitors are pouring in to see for themselves the incredible "swinging London" that has sprung up overnight. Famous film stars, such as Madonna and Hugh Grant, have chosen to live in the grooviest capital in Europe. Where else can you see such a host of cutting-edge attractions as the Millennium Dome, the London Eye, the Tate Modern and, er, the Jubilee Line? No wonder film stars like Madonna are flocking from all over the world to see Hugh Grant on the London Eye or to enjoy a cafe latte in one of the famous pavement cafes of Notting Hill.

But let us not forget that London is an overcrowded city in a small and overcrowded island, cursed with a transport system that would have disgraced the Middle Ages. There simply isn't room for all these foreigners to come over here, gawping at our art exhibitions and claiming social security.

Mr Hague and Ms Widdecombe are surely right when they say an enormous prison should be built to house all these unwanted visitors to our shores. *(Surely this is the wrong editorial? Ed.)*

Tate Modern

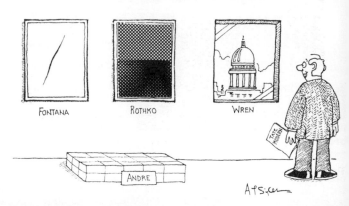

FONTANA   ROTHKO   WREN

ANDRE

TRACEY EMIN
Private View

WHO ARE THEY?
Ken's New Team To Run London

Jenny Gavroche, 51, divorced wife of millionaire media mogul Lord Mirabelle. Jenny, who lives in Haringey, sits on over 100 advisory bodies, task forces, review groups and non-governmental organisations, including the North London Sandwich Board, the Traffic Lights Authority and the Fish and Chips Licensing Agency and is Deputy Chair of Friends of the Archway Footbridge Trust. Jenny is to be Ken's No. 2 as Vice-Mayor.

Winji Hatterjee, 41, high-flying race relations expert with special brief for race relations at the Lambeth Institute for Race Relations. Winji recently described the Duke of Edinburgh as "a fascist mass-murderer who in a civilised society would be taken out and macheted to death". He is to be Ken's race relations supremo in charge of rooting out racism in the race relations industry.

Ken Cruiser, 22, known as "Green Ken", has been a lifelong member of the Green Party and has worked as Chief Environmental Co-ordinator on Tower Hamlets Council's Table Tennis and Snooker Sub-Committee. Ken is a passionate believer in burning cars to solve the capital's pollution problems, and is also a keen gay.

Lord Tape, 66, known as "Red Tape". Lib Dem high-flyer, formerly chair of Tooting Bec Council Bicycle Tracks and Canal Towpath Restoration Committee has turned down Ken's offer to run London transport because, he says, "I cannot agree with Ken's policy on Chechnya." *(That's enough New Team. Ed.)*

NEW-LOOK KEN AND NEW-LOOK QUEEN

I humbly submit to your gracious Majesty, Ma'am

You're a diamond geezer, mate!

Eye Poll: Should Ken replace the Duke of Edinburgh?

YESTERDAY IN PARLIAMENT

Presenter: The main business in the Commons yesterday was a heated debate on the right of female MPs to breast-feed in the Chamber.

Ms Patsy Jacket *(Nusildon, Lab)*: Ms Speaker, it is an outrage that, at the beginning of the 21st century, I am not allowed to breast-feed my baby during debates. What kind of example are we setting to the rest of the country, when a supposedly modern Government like Tony's can't even allow a basic human right to be exercised in the legislative chamber of the Unmarried Mother of Parliaments?

(Tory cries of "Get your tits out for the Labs!")

The late Alan Clark *(for it is she)*: Bit of a scrubber but I wouldn't mind taking her round the jumps?

The Speaker *(Mrs Boothroyd)*: You're dead, so keep quiet. Ms Jacket, I have told you before that I will not have public displays of mammarian apparatus in this Chamber. So, kindly fasten your blouse.

(Tory cries of "Shame!")

Presenter: Meanwhile the House of Lords was electrified by a contribution from Lord Barg of South Bank.

Lord Barg: Good evening and welcome to tonight's speech by myself. As noble lords will know, I am a very important person, and that now I am a working peer, I am even more important. Not that I can afford to spend much time here in the House of Lords (except for lunch obviously) because I have a very important job outside this House, as I may have mentioned before.

That is why, if we are to drag this House into the 21st Century that Tony Blair has led us into, two reforms are absolutely vital.

The first is that, if important people like me are to be expected to come here, we should be paid at least £10,000 a day.

And secondly, when we get here, we should be given proper modern facilities, such as phones, faxes e-mails, etc, so that we can conduct our very important outside business, such as setting up interviews with major international artists such as Dolly Parton and "Posh Spice".

But that's enough of the more staid world of Westminster. The real political excitement nowadays is to be found in the devolved chambers in Scotland and Wales. In Edinburgh yesterday the MSPs moved a motion of censure on Donald Dewar for only providing Dundee Cake in the Scottish Parliament cafeteria.

Joyce McWhingie *(East Kiltshire, SNP)*: Mr Presiding Officer, it is an outrage that, at the beginning of the 21st Century, the only cake offered to members of this Parliament is Dundee, an unrepresentative cake from a single Scottish city. What kind of message is this giving to our constituents in the rest of Scotland? I tell you, there are perfectly good cakes which come from Auchtermuchty, Bannockburn, Rockall and every other part of this great nation of cake-makers.

(Cries of "Death to the English!", "Braveheart forever!")

Presenter: Meanwhile, in Cardiff there was an angry exchange when a Plaid Cymru AM, Hugh Davies, accused Lib Dem David Hughes of not speaking in Welsh when he wished him good morning in the toilet.

Huw Davies *(Cwm Rhondda, PC)*: Pwllgwn-gychllanrobllantsyliogogoch...

FM's "Music To Send You Back To Sleep While You're Eating Your Breakfast" Show, with Sid Wagner.)

The Literary Sensation of the Millennium!

What You Missed

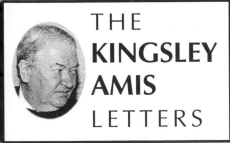

THE KINGSLEY AMIS LETTERS

The world of one of England's

greatest literary figures of all time at

last revealed in its raw, thrusting,

visceral *(Get on with it. Ed.)*

Letter 365

To Philip Larkin

12 Oct 1968

Dear Old Bumface,
Did you see that piece in The Times by that dreadful leftie Rees-Mogg[1]? What a load of bum. Must go now. Feeling a bit pissed.
Yours, Kingers

[1]This is a reference to Lord "Bill" Deedes, long-serving editor of the Daily Telegraph and a Cabinet minister in the second administration of Pitt the Elder (1756-61).

Letter 978

To The Editor of The Times

10 April 1975

Dear Sir,
How can your views on anything be taken seriously when, in a leader on the future of education, you use a hanging participle in conjunction with a gerundive, unsupported by any clausal noun? What a leftie bastard you must be!
Your humble and obedient servant,
K. Amis
The Garrick Club, WC2.

PS. You can cut the last bit if you like! I was a bit pissed when I wrote it.

Letter 979

To Philip Larkin

10 April 1975

Dear Bumface,
I have just written a brilliant letter to The Times about the complete collapse of standards in their pages. I don't suppose they'll print it, being a bunch of lefties! I gather Rees-Mogg is a Jew to boot. Not sure about that last bit. I'm a bit pissed.
Bum, bum, bum,
Kingers

'The Collected Letters Of Sir Kingsley Amis OM' is published in three volumes by Fishwick & Tweed, £299.99.

My first day at school

by William Hague

9.05 am: Refused to sit next to the gypsy children from behind the estate because they smell, and demanded Mrs Rourke immediately remove them instead to a secure classroom with no windows.

9.27 am: Unfairly sent to the headmaster's office for using reasonable force to defend my box of Crayolas from being viciously borrowed.

9.40 am: Made leader of the Conservative Party.

HEL-LEO!!!

by Our Entire Staff

NOT SINCE the year 0 A.D. has the birth of a baby so captured the imagination of the entire world!

For a few magical hours, the human race was able to put all its divisions on one side, to forget all its cares and its woes, the starving millions in Africa, the dead bodies in the killing fields of faraway Chechnya, and instead raise a glass of good cheer to the miracle of new life – the cutest tot on Planet Earth. *(Keep going, this is brilliant! Ed.)*

And in this sacred moment, which had the power to transform us all, a tough, hardened politician became a doting Dad.

There was scarcely a dry eye in the whole of Britain, as millions of readers forgot their Frosties and their Golden Grahams to gaze in silent homage at Sir Paul McCartney's daughter's pictures of little, laughing Leo, as he took his first shy peek at the baffling world of 2000 A.D.

What will he make of it, the world of the Internet, the Millennium Dome and Tate Modern?

And what will he think of us, his fellow travellers on a global voyage into the unknown, as we struggle to fill up hundreds of pages with this mind-numbing drivel?

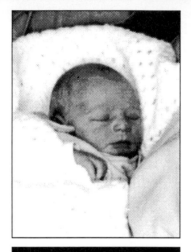

ON OTHER PAGES

● **What Happens When A Baby Is Born?** A Doctor states the obvious. **2**

● **What Cherie Must Be Feeling** – A psychiatrist takes the money **3**

● **To Breast Feed Or Not To Breast Feed?** Hundreds of hackettes debate the most burning issue of our age **4**

● **What Happened When I Had My Baby** – Hundreds more hackettes bore us to death with their childbirth experiences **5**

● **Why I Don't Want A Baby** – Deirdre Spart explains why she refuses to add to the population explosion **6**

● **Is Leo A Leo?** Asks our top astrologer Mystic Mogg **7**

● **Will Leo Support Man U?** by Our Sports Editor Sally Jockstrap **8**

● **Will Baby Blair Win The Next Election?** by Our Political Staff Charles Moore-Babyplease **9**

● **How Sir Paul's Girl Landed The Photo-Scoop of the Millennium 10**

● **How We Put Our World-Beating Baby Leo Supplement Together** – a behind-the-scenes look at the birth of a great news feature **11**

PLUS thousands of pictures of a baby **11-94**

If you would like to see more pictures of Baby Leo just click onto our special website — www.gorgeousbaby.co.uk

STOP PRESS

ENGLAND TRIUMPH IN TEST

Final score: England 571-1 dec. Rumbabwe 14 and 7-9

Play stopped when ground was occupied by war veterans of Rumbabwe Patriotic Liberation Front wielding machetes and demanding the right to plant genetically-modified mealie-mealie on the square.

WHO WILL BE BABY LEO'S GOD-PARENTS?

You decide on who should give Tony's tot spiritual & moral guidance in the years to come

Godfathers

Ant and Dec
Alain de Botton
Martin McGuinness
Martin Clunes
Bob Ayling
Vladimir Putin
Jamie Oliver
The Very Reverend Richard Chartres, Bishop of London

Godmothers

Britney Spears
Dr Germaine Greer
Sister Wendy
All Saints
Martha Lane Fox
A.S. Byatt
Joanna Lumley
Rabbi Julia Neuberger

An Eye Phone Line Special 0898 742346757

PROTEST AS QUESTION TIME 'DUMBS DOWN'

by Our Media Staff **Lois Common-Denominator**

CRITICS of the BBC were furious last night at the invitation of "Boy" Charles to appear on the prestigious current affairs programme "Question Time".

Said one, "What on earth was a politician doing on this programme amidst all the heavyweight figures from the world of entertainment?

"Boy Charles," continued the critic, "was out of his depth with guests like George O'Dowd on the show. And who cares what he thinks about the Euro compared to panellists like Joanna Lumley, Ant and Dec or Graham Norton?"

(Cont'd. p. 94)

ST CAKES HEAD LASHES OXBRIDGE

by Our Education Correspondent **Lynda Chalk**

TOP INDEPENDENT school head Mr R.G.J. Kipling of St Cakes School For Boys (Motto: "Exceedingly High Fees") hit out today at the Oxbridge admissions system which denies opportunities to "thick boys".

Kipling singled out the case of one of his high-paying *(Surely "flying"? Ed.)* pupils Crispin St John de Plankke who with one E grade "A" Level in Classical Civilisation was told "not even to try" for the prestigious Nuclear Physics course at Balliol College Oxford.

"The lad has got it all going for him," said Kipling. "He's a bloody nice bloke, he is in the school First XV and his father is a friend of mine. Yet they turned him down. There must be something wrong with a country that discriminates against its young people solely on the grounds of intelligence."

A-LEVEL PLAYING FIELDS

Yet within days of his rebuff by Balliol, de Plankke was offered a place on the Dome's training course learning to stack chairs in the Education Zone.

Says Kipling, "It has taken a foreigner, Mr P.Y. Gerbeau, to recognise the potential of a British youngster whilst the Oxbridge dons in their ivory towers spend their days drinking port and talking to each other in Latin."

P.Y. Gerbeau is 39.

PRESCOTT JOINS DEBATE

You don't have to be clever to get to the top

QUEEN AND PRINCE PHILIP

Will They Re-Marry?

by Our Court Staff **Major Ron Knee**

THERE was speculation last night that Her Majesty The Queen and the Duke of Edinburgh might re-marry.

For many years the couple have lived separate lives with the Duke spending much of his time abroad.

Recently, however, the Queen (73) and her consort have been spending more and more time in one another's company.

Only last week they were spotted by millions of people opening the new pedestrian bridge over half of the River Thames.

WE DO

A palace insider told me: "They have a lot in common and they are more mature than they were 50 years ago. Obviously, both of them are keen to set an example of stable family life to their children."

I'm not going to exploit you

You must think I was born yesterday

ROY of the REDS

UNITED'S FORM HAS SUFFERED A SLUMP

THE BOSS NEEDS MORE COMMITMENT

I WANT TO SEE REDS ALL OVER THE PARK

HURRAH!

THE THIRD THIS WEEK

COME ON YOU REDS

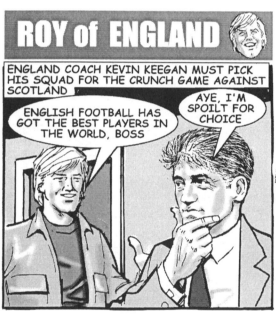

ROY of ENGLAND

ENGLAND COACH KEVIN KEEGAN MUST PICK HIS SQUAD FOR THE CRUNCH GAME AGAINST SCOTLAND

ENGLISH FOOTBALL HAS GOT THE BEST PLAYERS IN THE WORLD, BOSS

AYE, I'M SPOILT FOR CHOICE

RIGHT LADS, THE TEAM SHEET IS UP

DE GOEY
STAM
DESCHAMPS
LE BOEUF
DI MATTEO
ZOLA
JUNINHO
KANU
FLO
GINOLA
BERGKAMP

ER... KEVIN... I THINK THERE'S A SLIGHT PROBLEM

ROY of the LOSERS

THIS NEW STADIUM DESIGN IS A DISASTER

IT'S ONLY SUITABLE FOR FOOTBALL

THEN WHERE ARE ENGLAND GOING TO PLAY?

MILLENNIUM BLAIR 'WOBBLES'

by Our London Staff
Paul Footbridge

THE NEWLY opened Millennium Blair, which aimed to bring together the North and South of the country, has developed a dangerous "wobble" according to its designer, Philip Gould.

Millions of people responded to the idea of the Blair with enormous enthusiasm and thronged in large crowds to get on it.

But when they finally reached the Blair they found themselves swaying around dangerously with every breath of wind.

Blair of Light

Said one disappointed Blair walker, "I lost my balance and had no idea where I was going. The Blair was swinging first to the left and then to the right. After a while I felt sick and had to go home."

The multi-million-pound Blair has now been temporarily closed pending an enquiry. Said architect Sir Alastair Campbell, "After the excitement of the fireworks surrounding its opening it was bound to be a bit of a disappointment. But there is nothing fundamentally wrong with it. After all, the Blair was designed for quite a bit of movement."

ON OTHER PAGES

Is Leo to blame?

Charles Moore takes a wry, sideways weekend look at the problems of buying coffee in Canary Wharf

TO THOSE of us who need an early morning beverage the advent of the new-style coffee emporia from the United States has brought a bewildering variety of choice. Whereas in former days one simply asked one's fag or mater to procure "an cup of coffee", one now has to request from the vendor a frighteningly accurate description of the precise quantity, style and ingredients of the desired brew – or face humiliation from the knowing employees of Mr Starbuck!

Thus, when I ordered "a smallish white frothy coffee with no whipped cream to take away in one of those cardboard beakers with a top, my good man", I was amazed when the young fellow behind the counter responded by laughing uncontrollably and pointing to the menu where the mysterious words "Short latte to go" were inscribed in (cont. p. 94)

LEGOVER VOTED WORLD'S MOST POPULAR PASTIME

by Our Leisure Correspondent **Sir Toy Strong**

A PANEL of experts voted Legover, invented in Denmark in 1956, as "the most enjoyable leisure activity in the world".

It is estimated that over 700 billion people have enjoyed Legover sometime in their lives.

FUN

This uniquely popular game is based on the principle of fitting two items into each other and then breaking them apart again.

Legover was voted a clear winner over all other past-times, way ahead of traditional rivals such as reading, ballroom dancing, walking the dog and listening to Melvyn Bragg on Radio Four.

Among the many famous addicts of Legover down the ages have been President John F. Kennedy, Elizabeth Taylor, the Duchess of York, Mr Robin Cook and Steven Norris.

Will Smith at Agincourt

At the Cinema

New Hollywood Releases

U-194

GRIPPING World War II story about how U.S. soldiers cracked the Enigma Code and won the war in the Atlantic with no help from the Royal Navy at all. Stars **Matt Damon** as Lieutenant Brad Hero and **Sir Alec Guinness** as Adolf Hitler.

Charge of the Light Brigade

STIRRING tale of how the U.S. Seventh Cavalry won the Crimean War by charging at the Turkish guns in the so-called Valley of Death. Stars **Bruce Willis** as Captain Chuck Nolan and **Sir John Mills** as the evil Ottoman Emperor, Salaman The Rushdie.

Zulu

EXTRAORDINARY tale of American heroism with **Tom Hanks** as leader of an isolated troop of Green Berets who single-handedly defeat the British Army in Zululand in 1879, thus ridding the world of slavery for ever. Watch out for cameo performance by **Stephen Fry** as the evil Michael Caine.

Henry Vth

WILL SMITH is the wise-cracking American General, Henry Plantagenet The Fifth Junior who, with his "Dirty Dozen" Special Forces archers, single-handedly defeats the evil British Army and liberates France from Anglo-Saxon tyranny, co-starring **Alan Rickman** as the wicked English Dauphin. *(That's enough terrible Hollywood history. Ed.)*

"I didn't know Legoland was a real country"

Prince Charming at 18 – Your Questions Answered

1. How do we address you, Your Majesty?
   Just call me charming!

2. What are your hobbies, sire?
   I like being charming, turning on the charm and charming people.

3. Are you a good cook?
   You should taste my four-and-twenty blackbirds baked in a pie! It's wicked! And, of course, charming.

4. Are you going to marry Snow Nose?
   I think you must mean Snow White, who is a good friend but no more than that.

5. What about the rumours concerning you and Cinderella Palmer-Tomkinson?
   "Snorters" and I are also just good friends.

6. Are you going to follow your father and join all the King's Horses and Men?
   I think I'll go to University first and read History of Charm, and then see how it works out.

7. Do you think you will live happily ever after?
   I've never really thought about it.
   (Continued for 94 years)

The Guardian's Cut-Out-and-Keep Guide To The Girls That Prince William Is Most Likely To Bonk

(Surely 'Guide To The Tragic Situation In Sierra Leone'? Ex-Ed.)

The Honourable Laetita Witherington-Montefiore-Strobes, 18. Eldest daughter of Lord and Lady Brideshead-Starborgling. Laetitia recently saw a photograph of the Prince in *Country Life*, which she cut out and pinned up in her bedroom next to a picture of her pony, Flapjack.

Tarara Boomdeay-Palmer-Cokehead, 27. Fun-loving partygoer and daughter of Brigadier Peter de la Boomdeay, Commander of His Excellency's Land Forces, Oman. Tarara met the Prince at the popular Slappers' Nightclub in Cheltenham at a fund-raising evening in aid of the United Kingdom Independence Party (UKIP).

Baroness Jay, 75. Although slightly older than William, the sexy leader of the House of Lords is known to be a good-time girl who likes clubbing, skiing and constitutional reform.

Julie Burchill, 53. Although they have never met, the self-styled Queen of the Groucho has all the attributes to become a modern Queen of England. She is a self-confessed drug addict, lesbian and writer for the Guardian (See the Hon. Polly Toynbee, 271).

Alan Rusbridger, 21. Handsome, bespectacled Harry Potter lookalike, would make a perfect companion for the young and impressionable future King of England. Like William, Alan is known to be keen on the internet and has his own website: rubbish@grauniad.zzzz

"Surprise!" HAPPY 18TH WILLIAM

A Hearse Driver writes

Every week a well-known taxidermist is asked to write about an issue of topical importance. This week **Morty Crem** (Hearse Number 74243) on the Funeral of the late Charles Kray.

Wonderful turnout eh guv? They done you proud, you were a real gentleman and no mistake you looked after your own and you loved your mum and woe betide anyone who said otherwise out with the shooter and bang in the face no nice to see Reggie there though why they had to cufflink him Gawd knows he's harmless now he couldn't even kill a fly though he might tear its wings off and make the little bastard eat them no it's a disgrace you know what I'd do with people like Reggie let him out that's the only language he understands I 'ad your brother Ronnie in the back of my hearse once another gentleman just like all of you they don't make 'em like you any more...

NEXT WEEK: The life of another vicious criminal warmly remembered.

MORE MONEY TO BE POURED DOWN DRAIN

by Our Millennium Staff **M.T. Dome**

THE WORLD's largest drain, situated in Greenwich and designed by world-famous drain architect Lord Rogers, is to receive a further £29 million boost, in tribute to its inexhaustible capacity for wasting huge sums of public money.

"The Drain is uniquely designed," explained Heritage Secretary Chris Smith, "so that you can you pour any amount of money down it, without any of it ever coming back."

BOTTOMLESS PIT

"We should be proud of the Drain," said leading drain expert Simon Jenkins. "No other country can claim to have wasted anything like this amount of money.

"Our early forecasts of £758 million passing through the drain have actually been exceeded. It looks as though we shall soon have reached the incredible figure of £1 billion. Truly we can be proud of Britain."

STOP PRESS

Drain Champion Honoured

FORMER Times Editor Simon Jenkins is to be ennobled for his services to the Millennium Drain, under the title of Lord Jenkins of Greenwich. Earlier this year Lord Jenkins published a widely-acclaimed book, "The 1000 Best Drains in Britain".

Alternative Rocky Horror Service Book

No. 94 Service For The Gender Realignment Of An Incumbent

The Bishop: A warm welcome to you all on this sunny *(or it may be rainy)* day!

All: Good morning, Barry *(or it may be Jim, Kevin or Tom)*.

Bishop: We are gathered here together to turn this man into this woman.

(Here the incumbent shall present himself for solemn realignment)

Bishop: Do you, John, agree to become Jane?

Incumbent: I do.

Bishop: And do you promise solemnly that you will remain faithfully as a woman as long as you both shall live?

Incumbent: We do, indeedy.

(There will then follow a reading from the Book of Genderless)

"Chapter One. And in the beginning God created male and female. Male and female created He them.

And the first man was called Adam. And the first woman was called Eve.

And Adam looked upon the woman and said 'I'd like to be you'.

And God saith unto them, 'There is no theological objection.'

So Adam became Eve and everyone lived happily ever after."

Here endeth the lesson.

Bishop: We were now going to sing a hymn.

All: Ha, ha, ha. We know what cometh next!

Bishop: But it's become a "her" instead.

All: Nice one, Barry *(or it may by now be Jemima, Gladys, etc)*

Bishop: Number 94, She Who Would Valiant Be.

THAT PETER JAY INTERVIEW IN FULL

A Private Eye digest service for readers too busy to read the 188 exclusive interviews in the Sunday supplements

Once he was hailed by Time magazine as the most promising... first-class brain... Winchester and Balliol... glittering prizes... Treasury high-flyer... prime minister's daughter... golden couple... ambassador to Washington at only 26... wife has legover with Watergate star... Jay has legover with nanny... love child... washed-up... TV-Am's Famous Five... Roland Rat... washed-up again... legover with some other people... Robert Maxwell's chief of staff... really washed-up this time... old friend Birt gives him job at BBC on £200,000 a year... never seen again.

Jay's monumental 94-part series *The Road To Nowhere, A History Of Trying To Make Money*, will be broadcast shortly on BBC Choice on alternate Tuesdays at 1.35 (subject to Indoor Bowls Championship from Leicester).

ZIMBABWE LATEST

I am now casting my vote

You don't have to, Boss, you're going to win anyway

Radio 4

Today Programme

What you didn't miss

John Humbug: So are you going to confront the Zimbabwean Delegation today over their attitude to white farmers?

Robin Cook: Well John, obviously I will be talking to the representatives of the government of Zimbabwe over the unacceptable treatment of . . .

John Humbug: But will you be tough with them? Will you tell them to stop it?

Robin Cook: Well not exactly, John.

John Humbug: Why not?

Robin Cook: Because I don't want them to pour petrol over my head, set fire to me and then chop me up with machetes.

John Humbug: Sorry, I think the line's gone... *(cont 94KHz)*

Zimbabwe Election Results

(continued from page 1)

Mugabe South (formerly Harare North)

Zanu-PF Elected

Mr Mbastard Machete (Zanu-PF) **3**;

Mr Aloysius Nhoper (MDC – Opposition Party) **7,317,402**.

Zanu Gain

100% swing to the Monster Raving Zanu Party of President Screaming Lord Mugabe.

"My goodness, Leylandi... how you've shot up!"

COURT CIRCULAR

HIGHGROVE

HRH the Prince of Wales will be the host at a special luncheon to mark the first official meeting between the Mistress Royal, Dame Camilla Parker-Knoll, and Her Majesty the Queen. The Mistress Royal has been prepared for this meeting through a course of instruction given by His Grace the Archbishop of Canterbury. Her Majesty will greet the Mistress Royal with a traditional frosty look of the type normally granted only to Her Non-Royal Highness the Duchess Fergiana. There will then follow an embarrassed and silent luncheon, at which the following dishes will be on the menu:

Chilled Windsor Soup
Cold Tongue Pie
Cold Shoulder of Mutton
Never-To-Be-Queen of Puddings

GATCOMBE PARK

HRH the Princess Royal will grant an exclusive interview to the Grocer Magazine in which she will praise the virtues of genetically-modified food-stuffs, and will describe their critics as "big-eared loopy weirdos living in Gloucestershire with their mistresses".

BUCKINGHAM PALACE

HRH the Prince Philip will add his two-pennyworth to the above debate, by describing genetically-modified organisms as "a bloody useful way to keep the natives fed when their bongo-bongo harvest fails." He will go on to describe critics of GMOs as "pathetic wimps who will never be king so long as I have anything to do with it".

Camilla And The Queen – Where Do We Go From Here?

By Lady Antonia Holden, the Lord Blake, the Lord St John of Fawningsley, Mr James Witless, Mr Ben Pimlotofrubbish and assorted other snobs and bores

THE historic meeting of Camilla Parker-Bowles and the Queen raises a number of important constitutional questions.

The first is do you want 1000 words or 2000?

The second is how much do we get? £2000 or £4000?

And the third is – is this enough? (No. Ed.)

No student of the complexities of British constitutional procedure can fail *(cont'd. p. 94)*

HISTORIC MEETING PT II

And how long have you been a slapper?

Ha ha ha ha, Your Majesty

MARRIAGE 'NOT ON THE CARDS'

by A.N. Idiot

DESPITE THE historic meeting between Camilla Parker-Bowles and the Queen, senior Buckingham Palace sources have sought to play down any talk of marriage.

"The Queen would of course have to first divorce Prince Philip," he said, "and the prospect of the first Royal lesbian marriage will inevitably upset many in the Church."

Privately though, he admitted the couple have met with the Archbishop of Canterbury who is seeking to smooth the way for their eventual union.

Daily Mail

PROFILE

The weird world of the right-wing nutcase

A SINISTER figure in a baseball cap, this man wanted to start a campaign of terror in London with a series of political bombshells that would spread fear and panic amongst the population. He targeted foreigners, gays and those he called "the liberal elite". Neighbours described him as "a bit of a Conservative leader" and when police raided his flat they found pictures of Mrs Thatcher all over the wall *(Are you sure this is right? Ed.)*

The Daily Hurleygraph

Friday, June 2, 2000

Yes, It's Over! Showbiz Couple To Split

By Our Entire Staff Hugh Grant-Montgomery Massingberd

THE LONG-running love affair between the glamorous actress and the floppy-haired public schoolboy is finally over.

For 11 years the beautiful Liz Hurley and the diffident Charles Moore were inseparable.

She was always to be seen on his front page and wherever Liz went Charles would be there faithfully reporting her every deed.

Their relationship even survived Charles's infidelity when he was caught with an older woman (the "Divine" Mrs Thatcher) as his lead story. The disgrace of his now infamous "sucking up" to this notorious woman shocked Liz deeply but somehow she forgave him and soon she moved back into his newspages, sucking a dummy, wearing a dress or putting on a pair of sunglasses.

But then suddenly this week came the devastating announcement – Liz was no longer an item. Fans could not believe that Charles had dumped Liz from the front page after only one day, and had been seen flirting with the idea of putting some news in his paper.

Daily Telegrant

A spokesman for the couple said there was no third party involved – although friends claim privately that the dashing Charles and the Conservative Party have recently been getting into bed together.

Charles Moore is the star of *Four Wedding Announcements and an Obituary* and *Notting Much Else.*

"Life is seldom that black and white, Mr Beardsley"

75

BBC TOTALLY HOPELESS SAYS BBC CHAIRMAN

by Our BBC Staff **Roland Ratings**

THE Chairman of the BBC, Sir Christopher Bland, today lashed out at himself.

In a scathing attack, he accused the BBC of producing nothing but mindless rubbish.

"Who's in charge?" he asked, at a specially convened press conference in his lavishly-appointed chairman's office on top of Broadcasting House.

"The whole thing is a shambles. Whoever's running it should be sacked."

When it was pointed out to Sir Christopher that the man responsible was none other than himself, he immediately agreed to stay on at a huge increase in salary.

Sir Pigling Bland is 78.

"Apparently, at the Groucho Club they have fifty different words for snow!"

THE WRITING ON THE WALL

THE STORY SO FAR: the distinguished novelist Mr Will Self has been asked by the Independent *to sit in an art gallery writing down whatever comes into his head. Now read on…*

Erm *(takes panic-stricken look at small knot of journalists, uncomprehending teenage girls, etc)*. Lunch was crap. I can feel the ball of ill-digested pâté de fois gras swivelling in my intestinal labyrinth like some searing oesophagal shotgun pellet. A fart cracks out of my tremulously over-loaded sphincter with whiplash poignance. Windful, windy wind, winding its way windily out of the steatopygous Grand Canyon of my buttocks. Um *(looks up to see the bouffant-haired figure of Mr John Walsh scribbling excitedly in a notebook)* I've been flung – of that much I'm certain – flung large amounts of money, spun a couple of times like a twist of mephitic, mephistophelean candyfloss and then slammed down here.

The first thing I'm aware of are the voices, those random snippets of nonsensical chat, fragments of a few irrelevancies irrelevantly realised in gaunt, dauntless chambers where I can't share them, er, "What's that bloke doing over there?", "Isn't this supposed to be an art gallery?", "Yes, we've stopped taking the *Independent* actually."

Yes… blotched-face gorgonzola-grouted gargoyles, swarthy, earthy, turfy, preposterously phallic noses dangling over the scrotal pouches of their cheeks…

"… Obviously this guy has been given too much money. Did you read his last one? Awesomely bad," they gawp. They're accomplished gawpers these two, gawping warpedly, sniggering at my suffering, sniffing at my socks, smiling at my dithering, er… how much longer do I have to sit here? Doesn't this place ever close?… *(Continued for 94 days)*

GOVERNMENT TO LAUNCH 'THIN CAMPAIGN'

by Our Media Staff **Jane Thynne**

THE Government last night announced a new drive to get "thin ideas" on to the front pages of newspapers and magazines.

"For too long," said spokesman for the Ministry of Women, Tessa Jowell, "the media have been obsessed with 'heavyweight' issues, expecting the government to come up with initiatives on the breakdown of the Northern Ireland ceasefire or the appalling mess in the NHS.

"What we need is some really thin stuff," she declared, "something terribly light and feeble instead of all those awful meaty problems that tend to dominate the news."

WILLIAM VOGUE

"That is why I have organised this Body Image Summit today in the hope of persuading the public that as a body, this government is a fat lot of good to *(cont. p.94)*

Birt's Ten-Point Plan For Crime

1. **All criminals will be divided into four separate directorates: Crime Resources, Crime Management, Crime Development, and Crime Talent.**

2. **All criminals will be expected to operate within a two-tier internal market, comprising those buying in crime and those selling out.**

3. **There will be an increased emphasis on regional crime, plus a separate 24-hour rolling crime facility, which will supply digital crime across the board.**

4. **Night-time crime will be rescheduled to occur mid-morning, with special crime slots introduced throughout the day to** *(That's enough Birt. Ed.)*

A Typical Crime Of The Type Lord Birt Will Not Investigate

A TOP executive working at a public corporation such as the BBC walks out of the building with a million pounds of licence-payers' money stuffed in the pocket of his designer suit – *in broad daylight.* **Whilst occupying the building this man destroyed nearly everything of value inside it and gave away the jewels to a well-known fence, Mr R. Murdoch. What can be done?**

BIRT SOLUTION: Reclassify this as a major achievement deserving a peerage.

The Daily Telegraph
Great Inventions Of The World

Edited by **James Dyson**

No. 94 The Daily Telegraph

IT WAS in 1742 that a young Dorset engineer called William Deedes was working with the famous George Stephenson on the invention of the steam locomotive. It was his job to find a sedative to assist the early passengers to sleep during what was then the terrifying experience of travelling at 3mph.

After a false start with a dry ham roll and beaker of Early Grey tea, Deedes hit upon the formula which we now know as the Daily Telegraph.

The first edition contained a crossword, a letter from a disgusted resident of Royal Tunbridge Wells, a copperplate engraving of Mistress Hurley attending the premiere of Mr Sheridan's new play "Four Nuptials and an Interment", plus an essay by Dr Samuel Boris Johnson defending the union.

It was an immediate success and generations of travellers have since used the Daily Telegraph as an effective aid to slumber.

Sadly, having failed to patent his invention, the young Deedes was forced to work for the rest of his 507 years as a junior reporter on the newspaper.

No. 95 The Partwork

This clever device for filling up newspapers was first *(continued next week)*

TWO NEW ZONES FOR DOME

by Our Showbiz Staff **Cecil B. de Millennium**

TWO exciting new zones are to open shortly at the Greenwich Dome in a new plan to attract more visitors to the ailing theme park.

The first, the Bonus Zone, will show visitors members of the management team being given large cheques in recognition of their failure. A huge cheque, forty feet long, will illustrate the role of the bonus in Modern Britain and will be carried by members of the Railtrack Board of Directors, led by Lord Birt of the BBC.

Another zone will be called the Nepotism Zone, which will show a dramatic recreation of the way Mr Ben Evans (full name The Honourable Benedict Twistleton-Blackstone), the son of Labour Peer Baroness Blackstone of the LSE, was given the job of running the Dome by mummy's friend Peter Mandelson, even though he had no relevant experience or qualifications.

EVANS ABOVE!

Said a spokesman, "The new zones show what Britain is best at – rewarding failure and encouraging sleaze. We are confident that they will attract millions of people demanding that we close down the Dome immediately."

Asylum Seekers
AN APOLOGY

IN RECENT weeks, in common with all other newspapers, we may have given the mistaken impression that the asylum seekers flooding Britain were evil, scrounging, layabout criminals interested only in milking Britain's over-generous benefits system.

We now realise in the light of the story in which a number of asylum seekers were put into a big lorry and left there to die, that nothing could be further from the truth. They are in fact simple folk desperate to achieve a better life for themselves and their families and who've become tragic pawns in a racket by ruthless, organised criminal gangs who seek to profit from human misery.

We would like to apologise unreservedly for any confusion caused and for any further confusion in the future when, on discovering that another lorry-load of illegal immigrants has made it through Dover, we immediately label those aboard as evil, scrounging layabouts and criminals interested only in milking Britain's over-generous benefits system.

© All Newspapers

SHOULD EDITORS TAKE BURCHILL?

YES says Alan Rubbisher.

Burchill: Gets up your nose

THE hysteria about the alleged dangers of taking Burchill have disguised the basic truth – taking Burchill is harmless fun. You just read a line and suddenly the whole world goes fuzzy. Words lose their meaning, nothing is important any more and you find yourself saying "This is terrific shit". OK, so Burchill's expensive (with a Fleet Street value of ten thousand pounds a word), but hey you only live once and if you're surrounded by boring articles like I am at the Guardian, then Burchill seems like a good idea.

NO says everybody else.

NEW OLD SAYINGS

No nose is good news

KNACKER TRIUMPHANT AS DANDO KILLER HELD

by Our Crime Staff **Phil Prisons**

A DELIGHTED Inspector Knacker of the 500-strong Dando Squad was "over the moon" yesterday that at last the killer of TV's Jill Dando is behind bars.

"All that we have left to do now," said Knacker, "is find some evidence, link it to the killer and present the case to a jury."

He continued, "It would be quite wrong for me to say anything at this stage of the proceedings except that he did it and this is his name and address."

EDITOR OBSESSED BY DANDO

by Our Media Staff **Phil Paper**

A LONE editor living in Wapping, only six miles away from the scene of the murder, was said to be "obsessed" by *Crimewatch* presenter Jill Dando.

Police found pictures of Dando plastered all over his newspaper and he wrote endless fantasy articles about her death.

Said one friend of the editor, "He is a bit of a nutter and did the same thing with Princess Diana and Freddie Mercury.

"We are all glad that he is safely behind his desk."

David Yelland is guilty until proved innocent.

Letters to the Editor

Our National Shame

SIR – It is no good blaming the soccer yobs. We are all guilty in this country of institutional hooliganism. Each of us is a thug under the skin. And which of us can put his hand on his heart and say that, having had 20 pints of top-strength Belgian lager, he too would not have thrown the first chair?

REV. JEREMY
VOLETROUSER
Ince

SIR – The Belgian police are quite right. The only message these thugs understand is extreme violence. I therefore propose that the next time there is an international football championship, every known football supporter in Britain should be rounded up – preferably using CS gas, water cannon and armed baton charges – and then incarcerated for the duration of the tournament. Only by such draconian methods can this cancer in our midst finally be stamped out.

DAPHNE MILDEW
Barmby

SIR – The rise of soccer hooliganism can be dated exactly to the 1960s and the onset of the so-called permissive society. In my view the cynicism, disrespect and amorality of that degenerate epoch, associated with such TV shows as Sir David Frost's *That Was The Week* and Dame Joan Bakewell's *Late Night Line-Up*, were to sow a whirlwind from which the chickens are now coming home to reap.

R.F.P. KIPLING
St Cakes School, Keown

SIR – There can be no doubt as to who is to blame for the outrageous scenes in Brussels. Men. The male inability to control violent and aggressive urges has been responsible for everything bad that has ever happened in the history of the world. Don't just take away their passports. Take away their testicles – and then we will hear no more from them.

DAME GERMANY GREER
Shearer (Via Fe-mail)

SIR – The blame for the disgraceful scenes in Belgium must lie fairly and squarely with one man, William Hague, whose shameless attempts to whip up mass-hysteria against the euro has now resulted in the all too predictable genocide we have now witnessed on the continent.

JACK STRAW
Macmanaman

SIR – Come off it. What's new? We've been here before. All through history the English have been notorious for travelling to the continent to commit disgusting acts of hooliganism – Agincourt, Waterloo, D-Day – the list is endless, as I have shown already in my best-selling book *The University Challenge Book of English Soccer Hooliganism* (Snipcock and Tweed, £25.99).

J. PAXMAN
Southgate

SIR – It is scarcely surprising that we have witnessed the scenes we have in Brussels, when Englishmen are forced to live in a country which gives no outlet to their natural sense of patriotism. St George's Day was abolished by an EU directive. Trafalgar Square has been renamed Nelson Mandela Plaza. Morris dancing has been outlawed by politically correct loony left councils. All that is left for our young men is to demonstrate their pride in their country by smashing a few chairs over the heads of foreigners.

UKIP PATEL
Scholes

"Any trouble — and you're out"

ANOTHER APOLOGY

IN recent weeks, in common with all other newspapers, we may have given the impression that the England football team, under the inspired leadership of Mr Kevin Keegan, had the finest chance since 1966 of winning a major championship. Headlines such as "King Kev Can Do The Biz", "Shearer Magic Will Bring Home The Silver" and "Becksie's Blitzkrieg Will Win World War Four" may have led readers to believe that the England squad had some chance of coming in the first two in their group.

We now realise that the national team was without doubt the worst bunch of talentless no-hopers ever to don an England jersey, and that, in the words of Alf Littlejohn (Cab No. 94 with flag of St George obscuring the windscreen), "they should all be strung up, guv, it's the only language they understand".

We apologise unreservedly for any confusion that may have arisen from any previous articles by our sports team.

This apology first appeared in 1970, and has been reprinted every two years since that date.

"He's an armchair hooligan"

SALLY JOCKSTRAP'S EURO 2000 DIARY

Sunday
I arrive in Copenhagen. There is no atmosphere at all for the opening match of England vs. the West Indies. But the good news is that Frankie Dettori looks fit to tee off for Australia.

Monday
I arrive in Buenos Aires where Euro 2000 fever has not yet caught on. But never mind, England's skiers are looking good for a place in the prestigious American Masters in Troon.

Tuesday
Henley and the atmosphere is electric for the first test between the Harlequins and favourites The Chicago Bears. My money is on Pete Sampras riding Coulthard. *(That's enough diary. Ed.)*

Eye Film Choice

Victory Over Germany

STIRRING tale of how the American football team won the World Cup in 1966, starring Mel Gibson as Captain Bob Moore Jr III who scored all four goals in the sensational 4-2 win over the hated English.

Also stars Tom Hanks as Nobby Stileburger and Julia Roberts as the team's cheerleader in love with Bobby Charleston (John Travolta).

SUNDAY TIMES IN LEVY HOAX ROW

by John Ditherow

LORD LEVY has complained that two employees of the Sunday Times have been guilty of fraudulently misrepresenting themselves.

Both, he claimed, had pretended to be journalists.

"At first I was fooled," Lord Levy said, "when they said they were bona fide reporters covering a big political story, but then they gave the game away when they admitted they were, in fact, desperate hacks working for Murdoch."

Hax Evasion

Lord Levy concluded, "These people should stop trying to fool the public and get on with filling up their paper with rubbish about How The Pharaohs Invented The Atom Bomb."

SPECIAL CHARITY AUCTION

Lot 94:
Famous Old Bag

THE SUNDAY GRIMES

THE SUNDAY GRIMES
Pot Investigates Kettle

BY OUR INSULT TEAM

A POT last night made sensational allegations against the well-known Lord Kettle, suggesting that he had consistently avoided "being white".

Said the pot (Mr Rupot Murdoch), "Make no mistake, Lord Kettle is totally black and covered in filth. He is not nearly as clean as he makes out."

However, Lord Kettle denied he had acted improperly.

"In the 1998/99 tax year," he said, "I devoted my life to charitable works among the Kettle community. I am whiter than white."

He continued, "But why don't you look at Rupot? He is the one who is really black and has been thoroughly tarnished by a lifetime's association with muck and dirt."

Speaking from his New York tax exile, Mr Murdoch countered: "Lord Kettle is a devious, untrustworthy and disreputable item of kitchen equipment. And I should know."

TOYS 'N' GAMES

SPECIAL PESSIMISTS' EDITION

SNAKES AND SNAKES

DICE NOT INCLUDED

SNAKES AND SNAKES

MIKE TURNER

Exclusive Serialisation in the Sunday Times

THAT WAS THE SCISSORS AND PASTE THAT WAS
– a complete history of putting books together very quickly

by Humphrey Carpenter

Chapter One

IT ALL began in 1959 when Scissors and Paste met at Oxford and a new type of book was born.

Scissors was sharp and provided a cutting edge.

Paste was the glue that held it all together.

Between them they made an unbeatable team that was to take the cosy world of English publishing by storm.

Chapter Two

YET IT was not until Scissors and Paste met Humphrey Carpenter in an editorial office in Bloomsbury that the world finally came to recognise their amazing talents.

A book could now be written by copying a lot of bits out of other books and stringing them all together.

"It was incredibly exciting to be part of this new movement," says Carpenter, "even though nobody bought the books.

"You really felt you were doing something new and unoriginal," he says, "and you were."

NEXT WEEK: How the coming of the photocopier spelt an end to the Scissors and Paste boom.

Taken from "That Was The Scissors and Paste That Was" by Humphrey Carpenter.

Yes, It's Liz v. Anna In The Final!

By Our Tennis Staff Charles Phwoar!

WIMBLEDON has never seen anything like it!

Two of the all-time great self-publicists yesterday slogged it out for five hours for the ultimate prize – the chance to see themselves half-naked on the front page of the Daily Hellograph. And the battle of the semi-nude lovelies was one of the closest that the Telegraph has ever seen.

Daily Notsteffigraf

On the one hand, there was the fabulous 19-year-old Anna Korlegova, who despite losing in the first round continues to dominate women's tennis by posing in her underwear.

On the other, the legendary 39-year-old Liz Girley who, despite losing Hugh Grant, continues to dominate women's tennis by watching the odd match.

Top Seedy

The big question in the mind of millions of fans was which of these non-tennis players would have the most staying power *(Surely 'most revealing dress'? Ed.)* to win tennis's most coveted prize?

In the end, after a thrilling marathon, the result was a draw. Editor Charles Moore put both girls on his front page, and on all the inside pages as well.

HARRY POTTER IS HERE AT LAST

by Phil Space

AFTER months of eager anticipation it's out at last – my piece about the new Harry Potter book. It's the fourth in a hugely successful series of pieces that I've written this morning.

And, after all the speculation, I can finally reveal the title: "Harry Potter Is Here At Last", which was a closely guarded secret until 5 minutes ago when I thought it up.

This time the essential ingredients of the piece are the same (boy wizard... Hogwarts... single mother in café... loads of money... American film...) but it's much longer with a new darker theme.

I'm now attacking the marketing men, the media hype, and the sell-out to commercialism.

There are even rumours that I might end the piece by killing off one of my favourite clichés – "It's magic" – by writing about "How the magic has gone" instead.

© *Phil Space (exclusive to all newspapers).*

OXFORD PRODIGY DISAPPEARS

by Our Academic Staff
D. Phil Space

THE 15-year-old child prodigy who recently finished his exams at Magdalen College, Oxford, has completely disappeared.

William Hague, described as "a political genius" at the age of eight was expected to go to the very top of his field and become Prime Minister but it is believed that the pressure of work became too much for him.

"William became depressed," said his tutor Mrs Margaret Thatcher of Somerville College, "and has gone into hiding. Nobody knows where he is but he has sent me an e-mail claiming to be leader of the Conservative Party."

Friends say Hague has chosen deliberate obscurity in a desire to avoid a life in the spotlight, and his disappearance has prompted questions about whether talented children as young as William should be allowed (cont. p. 94)

LONDON   NEW YORK   TOKYO   BIOLOGICAL

—PILBROW—

BLAIR SHOCK AS SON HITS BOTTLE

by Our Entire Staff

WE CAN exclusively reveal that the son of the prime minister of England was last night found flat on his back, unable to stand up or even to speak.

It was clear that he had been sick and had been at the bottle for much of the evening.

When asked to identify himself he could only make incomprehensible gurgling noises.

Yet it soon became apparent that this was none other than Leo Blair. This must surely be the most embarrassing *(continued page 94)*

Teenage Drunkenness
Dr Utterfraud writes

AS A DOCTOR I am often asked "Can you dash off 800 words because we've just heard about the prime minister's son?"

The simple answer is "Yes, of course I can, though I'll have to ask for a double fee because it's short notice and my wife's got a ticket for the Centre Court."

What happens in most cases is that the teenager who has just finished his exams goes up West with a few mates and consumes a large amount of beer in a very short time.

The inevitable side-effect is that the patient is arrested, taken to the police station, where he gives a false name and is then plastered all over the media for the next 48 hours.

There is no known cure for this condition, which we doctors call... this isn't one of my best – can't I just write about Pete Sampras's ankle instead? *(No. Ed.)*
© A. Doctor.

GLENDA SLAGG
Every Reader's Worst Nightmare!

SO, EUAN got drunk? So what!? He's sixteen, for cryin' out loud! Haven't we all been there, done that, and bought the puke-stained t-shirt!?! Geddit?!? I once spent four days lying in the gutter outside El Vinos – and that was last week!?!?!? So, leave him alone, Mr Pressman, he's only a normal kid doin' what every kid in Britain is doing every day!?!?! Cheers, Euan!!!! Have one for the road?!??! (Geddit?!?!)

EUAN BLAIR??? Doesn't he make you sick!?!?!? What a disgrace to his mum and dad – not to mention the whole country whom he has shamed by his yobbish drunkenness??!? Forget the on-the-spot fine, Tony, take your belt to him and knock some old-fashioned sense into the little hooligan before he starts World War Three?!?!

CHERIE BLAIR?! – Doesn't your heart go out to her??? Her father was a drunken swine – and now her son has turned out the same!?!?! Take a tip from Auntie Glenda, Cherie – pour yourself a large one and drink all your troubles away!?!?!

I BLAME Cherie Blair!!?!? A young vulnerable boy is found lying in the gutter in a seedy London Square. Who knows what danger lurks nearby?? And where is his mother!?!!? Sunning herself in swanky Portugal without a care in the world for her home-alone littl'un whose cry for help, "Mummy, Mummy, I want my Mummy," went unheard. You should be ashamed of yourself!?!?! *(So should you. Ed.)*

HATS OFF to Tony Blair who has faced a week of hell with dignity and composure!?!?! There isn't a parent in the land whose heart doesn't go out to him in his hour of trial and tribulation???! He has set an example to us all not by reaching for his belt and giving his son an ill-deserved hiding, but instead by offering mature calmness and saintly compassion for his prodigal son!?!?!God bless you, Tony, and I shall personally drink your health many times tonight in El Vinos!!!!?!

TONY BLAIR – call yourself a dad??!? Where were you the night Euan went out with his so-called mates??! I'll tell you, Tony – you were out a-winin' and a-dinin' with your so-called mate, Lord Levy. What sort of an example is that setting to the nation's youth??!?! I blame the parents! Why doesn't Mr Blair senior come up to town and take his belt to his errant son!?!?!

HERE THEY are, Glenda's Summer Bar-B-Cuties!

SIR PETER JAY – TV's Mr Economics! OK, so everyone's turning your programme off, but you're turning me on!! I bet your hat's the only thing that's floppy!?!?!

JAMIE OLIVER – So you're married!?!?! Who cares!?!?! That's the way I like them – Glenda's Recipe for Love is like Risotto – it takes 20 minutes!?!?! Mmmmm!?!?!?!?

PAT RAFTER – He may have lost the men's singles on the Centre Court, but he could be a winner at mixed doubles round at my place!!! Geddit?!?!?

Byeeeeeee!!?!???!

"It's all gone Blair-shaped"

I'm going to get plastered

All over the newspapers

81

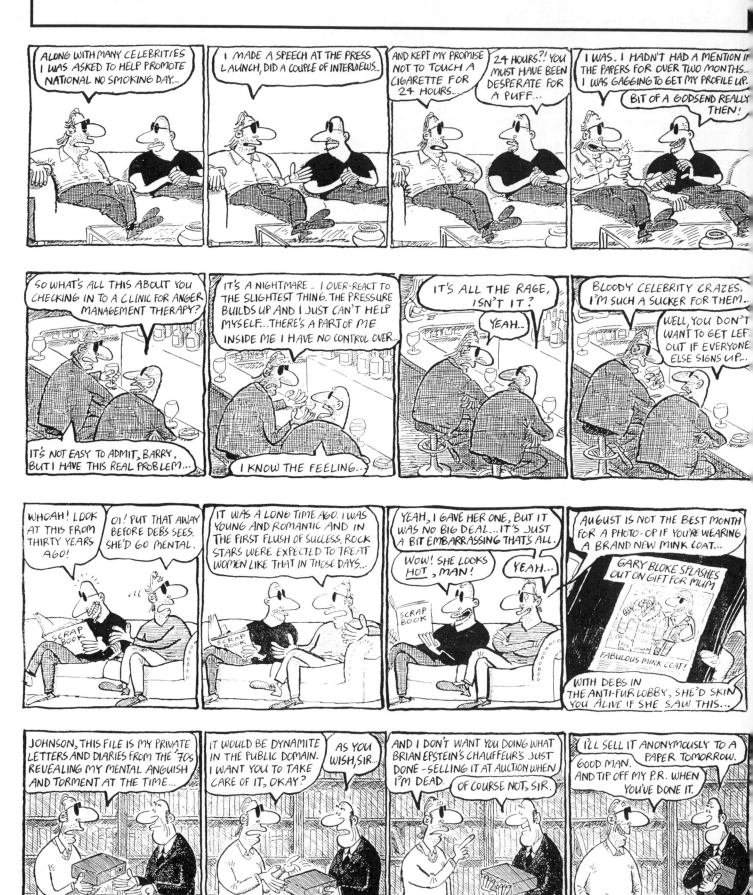

POLLY FILLER is off sunning herself in faraway Tuscany (lucky her!), so yours truly has been asked to step into the breach.

And if you're expecting a sideways look at domestic life from a woman's point of view, you're going to be seriously disappointed. That's Polly's patch and you won't catch me trespassing on it!

So, there I was sitting watching the Tweenies with my toddler Ivan (the terrible, as he's known in the Day-Relief household!!) when the phone rang and the features editor asked me to stand in for Polly.

"OK," I said. "I'll do it so long as I can get my hopeless partner Stephen to look after Ivan for half an hour."

Unfortunately, the aforementioned hopeless Stephen was too busy surfing the net hoping to catch a glimpse of the ex-nun on the toilet on the Big Brother website, so I had to leave Ivan with the Kurdish au-pair.

She speaks no English (of course!) and can't even stop Ivan throwing Chicken Run Pasta Shapes at her face! Talk about zero childcare skills!

So I have to admit to being somewhat distracted while I type out these words – and if they arrive covered in tomato suce, you can blame the feeble Azmal!! You'd think, by the way, a 16-year-old refugee would be grateful to join a friendly family with a charming toddler and brush-up on her ironing skills, but oh no, she prefers to cry all the time and phone home once a month!!!

As if that wasn't enough, I've just given up smoking! And I'm on a diet! And I'm pregnant! And I'm writing a novel. But more of that next time!

Polly Filler is on holiday.

"Stands the church clock at ten to three? And is there marching still at Drumcree?"

TONY BLAIR
An Apology

IN THE LIGHT of Tony Blair's decision not to allow us to take photographs of his family holidays, we, in common with all other newspapers, may have given the mistaken impression that Blair was a nutty, Howard Hughes-style, privacy-obsessed recluse. A man who is obsessively driven to hide his family away from the understandable desire of the press to share with the Country the Prime Minister's holiday hideaway.

We now realise, in light of Tony Blair's decision to allow us to take the photos, that Tony Blair is in fact a shameless publicity-seeking media whore, only too happy to offer up what should be a private family occasion in an obviously pathetic attempt to curry favour with the British press.

We would like to apologise for any confusion caused, and apologise in advance for Jason Fraser's charming snaps of Cherie Blair breastfeeding. © All Newspapers

OFFICIAL HOLIDAY PICTURE

Is that tower leaning, or am I pissed again?

The Road To Riches

Presented by Sir Peter Jaybotham

Part 94: Why People Want More Money

(Man in floppy white hat seen walking towards camera on Great Wall of China)

Sir Peter Jaybotham *(for it is he)*: It was here on the Great Wall that in the fourth Millennium BC the Emperor Ban King had the idea of the world's first cash-point. It was literally a "hole in the wall"!

(Cut to Jay looking at grass-skirted dancers on Tahiti giggling inanely at his hat)

Jay: Here in the Pacific Ocean they only had grass walls, which were no good for cashpoints. So they decided to use the coconut as their currency, since these could be easily obtained by shaking the branches of the local palm trees.

(Shot of coconut falling on head of Jaybotham, knocking off silly hat and rendering presenter unconscious. Cut to Jaybotham sitting in cafe outside the Colosseum with Lord Hattersley)

Jay: So much for the Emperor Diocletian. Now, Roy, you know a bit about money, having earned a lot of it in your time.

Hatterjee: Yes, indeed, Peter. Is this lunch on the BBC?

NEXT WEEK: The Great Depression, as viewers realise there are eight more programmes like this to go.

THE BEANO

BORIS the MENACE

WATCH THIS, READERS! I'M GOING TO USE MY COMIC TO HAVE SOME FUN WITH MR BLAIR! HA! HA! HA!

JUST A PUFF!

PTING!

OW!

YIKES!

FOR MY NEXT TRICK, CHUMS, I'M GOING TO MAKE A REAL STINK! CHORTLE! SNIGGER!

POOH! WHIFF! WHO THREW A DAILY TELEGRAPH IN HERE?

AND NOW — MY BEST WHEEZE OF ALL! I'M GOING TO RUN FOR PARLIAMENT AND DENOUNCE MR BLAIR'S POLICIES ON EUROPEAN MONETARY UNION! SMIRK! SMIRK!

VOTE 4 BORIS & BEANO

WHY YOU...!

GRR! I'LL TEACH YOU TO MAKE A FOOL OF ME, BORIS!

TIME FOR THE TRUSTY 'COMIC DOWN THE BACK OF THE SHORTS' ROUTINE, PALS!

HERE'S A 'SWING' YOU WON'T LIKE!

OWW! YAROO! THE SPECTATOR'S TOO THIN TO HELP! CRIPES! LUMMEE! ETC. ETC.

BILLY THE 'SWIZZ'

LOOK AT BILLY RUN!

YES, HE'S MILES BEHIND!

I AM. I'M GOING NOWHERE — FAST!

I THOUGHT YOU WERE MEANT TO BE FAST, BILLY!

PLUS ON OTHER PAGES

MICHAEL the MINX

LET'S PLAY FOLLOW THE LEADER — ME!

ANNIE the TERRIBLE

LOCK 'EM UP, EH, PALS!

JK

AND ALL THE OTHER TORY NUMBSKULLS!

100 YEARS OF QUEEN MOTHER CELEBRATIONS

by Our Royal Staff PHIL SPACE

EXACTLY one hundred years ago, Britain began celebrating the Queen Mother's centenary.

It barely seems possible that the Queen Mum's birthday has gone on for so long.

But it is true. It all began with a simple church service, leading onto a fly-past and a pageant, a tattoo, a family party, another fly-past, an unofficial celebration, an official celebration, Vera Lynne, Charlotte Church... And a hundred years on this remarkable catalogue of events is still going strong.

And the most amazing thing is how much Britain has changed since the Queen Mother's birthday celebrations began!

Way back then the Labour Government was still popular. The silver scooter had not been invented. England was hotly tipped to win Euro 2000. And Vanessa Feltz was still over 20 stone.

The Queen Mother can look back at an extraordinary century of tributes and her loyal admirers can look forward to another hundred years of *(That's enough. Ed.)*

Daddy's worried that you're going to live to a hundred as well

EXCLUSIVE TO THE OBSERVER

Is This The World's Most Evil Woman?

by Antonia Holden
(author of 'The Prince Charles I Never Knew' and 'Was Shakespeare A Writer?')

TO THE OUTSIDE world she is a benign, smiling old lady in a flowery hat, waving graciously to the adoring crowds.

But few people, apart from myself, are aware that this gentle granny in the long white gloves is perhaps the most machiavellian figure in the whole of twentieth century history.

For years, historians have claimed that the Queen Mother was a reluctant Queen, who only took the throne when there was no option, following the abdication of Edward VIII.

But hitherto undiscovered papers, so secret that even I have not seen them, reveal:

● The Queen Mother personally forced the Duke of Windsor to abdicate by blackmailing him with compromising photographs of him and Noel Coward in a gay bar in Berlin.

● The Queen Mother then forced her husband to be king,

making George VI so terrified of her that he became a compulsive smoker and died a premature death at the age of 31. Furthermore, he developed a serious speech impediment whenever she came into the room.

● The Queen Mother signed a secret treaty with Hitler, offering him the British throne if she could be his queen.

● The Queen Mother forced her daughter to marry the Duke of Edinburgh in 1947 against her will, in order to forge a dynastic alliance with the fascist regime of the Greek colonels.

● The Queen Mother was seen driving a white Fiat Uno through the streets of Paris on the fateful night of August 31st 1997.

All this, in my view, goes to prove that no more loathesome figure has ever disgraced the pages of the Observer. *(Surely history? Ed.)*

'QUEEN MUM WON'T SPOIL OUR DAY' say IRA Men

by Our Royal Staff
Jenny Bombed

ONE OF the most colourful and ancient ceremonies in the history of these islands, the "Planting of the Bombs", went on uninterrupted yesterday, despite threats by the Queen Mother to stage a "birthday party" in the middle of London.

As the sun shone down from a cloudless sky, vast crowds gathered round London's railway and tube stations, hoping to catch a glimpse of a train.

Ealing Tragedy

But nothing could deter the gallant men of the 7th/12th Omagh and Inniskillen Bombardiers (London Brigade) as, dressed in their full traditional uniform of balaclavas, dark jackets and boots, they re-enacted the age-old ceremonies of "Placing the Semtex" and "Causing the Chaos".

It was all performed with perfect timing, even though the Queen Mother had issued a warning that she intended to interrupt their proceedings by mounting a "spectacular", involving women, children and Norman Wisdom.

Wrong Type Of Bomb On Line

A spokesman for the "I Can't Believe It's Not The IRA" said last night, "It was a great day for us, and we're all delighted that it went off with a bang. Unfortunately, no one was hurt."

"You say the victim was attacked with a bread-knife..."

THE ALTERNATIVE VOICE

Dave Spart, Professor of Ideological and Semiological Entymology at the University of Barking (formerly Tower Hamlets Polytechnic)

Er... the sickening sycophancy that has subsumed the entire media press and the media er... on the occasion of the 100th birthday of the so-called

Queen Mother is totally sickening what has this toothless old parasite in a flowery hat ever done for the starving people of Rwanda, let alone the millions of people in this country who are officially below the poverty line er... this decrepit old harridan (incidentally a known fascist) totally symbolises the outmoded crumbling and totally decadent institution that is the Royal Family, ie the Monarchy, as no less an authority than Julie Burchill has pointed out "what a fat old bag" and as Tom Paine in his seminal piece in the Guardian last week observed "I hate *(cont. p. 94)*

This piece is reprinted by kind permission of the New Statesman Blind Trust, prop. G. Robinson, a totally sickening corrupt capitalist who pays our wages. *(Surely shome mishtake? Ed.)*

That Liverpool Citation in Full

SALUTAMUS CILLAM NIGRAM, NATA CANDIDA, FAMOSAM PERSONALITATUM TELEVISIONIS PER MULTOS ANNOS. OLIM PUELLA IN LIVERPUDLIENSIS, ORNAMENTUM SCENA MERSEYENSIS IN DECADO SWINGENSIS LX ET STELLA CAVERNI CUM LEGENDARIUS FABULOSUS QUATTUOR, AUT MOPPI TOPPI, JOHANNES, PAULUS, GEORGIUS RINGOQUE. SED CELEBRATISSIMA PER POPULARISSIME SPECTACULO TELEVISIONE IN HISTORIA, VIDELICET "CAECUS DATUS" IN QUO TRES JUVENES INTERROGANTUR AB STUPIDE PUELLA QUI SELECTAT UNUM PER VACATIONE LIBRA IN BALIENSE AUT CLEETHORPIBUS. DICIMUS TIBI "LORRA LORRA" HONORES ET FELICITATES, CHUCKA SCOWSA!

EVERYONE HAS RIGHT TO SUE EVERYONE ELSE
Shock Court Ruling

by Our Legal Staff **Joshua Rosenbeard**

UNDER a new ruling from the European Court of Human Rights, the "right to sue" has now been indelibly enshrined in British law for the first time.

A judgement by the 87 judges of the ECHR, representing every country in the Eurovision Song Contest, lays down the "fundamental right of every citizen to sue anyone they want for anything they feel like".

This follows several recent cases referred to the Court, including:

● **Mr X**, who sued the British prison authorities for keeping him in gaol after he had admitted murdering his wife. He was awarded £764,000.

● **Mrs B**, who sued the Happy Eater restaurant after she spilled one of their chocolate ice-creams over her new dress. She won £1,212,000.

● **Mr Y**, who sued a well-known shoe manufacturer after he tripped over one of his shoe-laces which he had forgotten to tie up, and stubbed his toe. He claimed there should have been a warning notice on the lace. The Court upheld his claim and awarded him £5,264,000.

● **Mr P**, a middle-aged homosexual, who sued the health service after he failed to become pregnant. The Court found that Mr P had been "discriminated against on grounds of gender" and awarded him £27,416,212.

● **Miss Z**, a teenager, who woke up one morning feeling "unhappy". She sued everyone she had ever known, and the Court awarded her all the money in the world in compensation – except for the amount owing to lawyers in the case which totalled £4.2 trillion for the three-year hearing.

If you would like to sue under the new Human Writs Act, contact Miss Cherie Booth of Fees-R-Us, c/o 10 Downing Street, London W1.

EXCLUSIVE TO PRIVATE EYE

THE TURDS
IN THEIR OWN WORDS

Spiggy: It was in 1963 that I had just got out of bed after several weeks. And that was the day we were going to record my new song 'Love is the thing. Hate isn't'.

Smudge: Actually, it was me that woke up that day. I had a chord in my head which turned out to be a whole song when George Martin got hold of it.

Krishna: Hari, Hari whilst stocks of the book last!

Ringo: Gordon puffed up to the top of the hill where the Fat Controller was pouring himself a large vodka and rolling an enormous spliff. "Hey, man!" he cried, as Thomas turned into a marmalade *(continued page 94)*

"Oh no – it's split-up"

CONCORDE – TECHNICAL SPECIFICATIONS

WING

PRAYER

ROBERT THOMPSON.

APOLOGY
The Concorde Airliner

IN COMMON with all other newspapers, we recently stated that, despite the crash of a French Concorde, this aircraft was probably the safest form of transport ever known to man, in addition to being one of the greatest triumphs of modern technology and the flagship of Anglo-French supremacy in world aviation. We pointed out that in 30 years the Concorde had a unique 100 per cent safety record, and that the cause of the French crash was a unique, billion-to-one chance which could never happen again in a million years.

We now accept that there was not a jot or scintilla of truth in these fanciful allegations, which we dreamed up in five minutes after a behind-the-scenes briefing by the PR department of British Airways. We now recognise that any aeroplane which can blow up just because of a simple tyre-burst is undoubtedly the most dangerous machine that has ever flown, and that, far from being a triumph of state-of-the-art technology, it is a ludicrously wasteful, environmentally destructive, clapped-out relic of the Sixties which should long since have been consigned to the dustbin of history.

© *All newspapers.*

DOME GREETS MILLIONTH VISITOR

A SMILING Mr P-Y Gerbil today welcomed the Millennium Dome's millionth visitor in the shape of Bailiff "Big Ron" Simmons of Simmons and Simmons.

Said Mr Simmons, "I have had a very enjoyable day looking around at the assets, but there is nothing here of any value."

Said Dome supremo Mr Gerbil, "This is a landmark in the history of the Dome and proof that we are still popular. We are expecting many more bailiffs in the next few weeks and shortly hope to welcome the official receiver himself."

Late News

MAZE PRISON TO BECOME ULSTER'S TATE MODERN

The empty Maze prison is to be redeveloped as "a cathedral of cool", said Northern Ireland Minister, Peter O'Mandelson. "Now that we have released all the prisoners that we've just put in there, it will make a superb setting for the contemporary artists of *(cont. p. 94)*

BIG BROTHER IS NOT BEING WATCHED BY YOU

EVERY night for the past three years, millions of viewers have been tuning in to one of the most bizarre experiments in public entertainment ever devised.

An ill-assorted group of unsavoury characters are forced to live 24 hours a day locked away from reality in a special "sealed environment" known as The Government.

These unpleasant, self-centred show-offs compete with each other to win the approval of the viewers, who at regular intervals can vote to have them evicted from the show.

STILL IN

Still the dominant personality of the group but losing ground fast is public-school educated **Tony**, nicknamed "The Vicar" for his smarmy, self-righteous manner in trying to ingratiate himself with everybody

Tipped by the bookies as the "dark horse" who could last the course the longest is **Gordie**, the dour, uptight Scotsman who "keeps himself to himself" and sits in a corner going through his cheque-stubs.

Viewers are all agreed that easily the most unpleasant female member of the cast is bossy, twice-married **Margaret**, known as "the Baroness". No one is keener on chucking people out, but she must herself now be a front-runner as next to be evicted, since no one has a good word for her.

Very much the odd man out of the gang is bluff, working-class **John**, a former ship's steward who is the butt of everyone else's cruel humour for his speech impediment. Viewers have a soft spot for the only member of the cast who seems to live in the real world.

ALREADY OUT

First to be given the heave-ho was bossy, middle-class smarty-pants **Harriet**, who got up everyone's nose by constantly sounding off on topics she knew nothing about.

Next to get the boot for his shame-less fanta-sising about dubious sexual escapades was Welsh-born **Ron**, the Clapham low-lifer whom no one was sorry to see the back of.

Third to get the thumbs-down was sharp-dressing man about Notting Hill **"Mandy"**, who was generally voted too clever by half. Amazingly, Mandy insisted that, despite getting the boot, he should be allowed back in, and Tony and the rest weakly agreed.

LATE NEWS • LATE NEWS • LATE NEWS • LATE NEWS

"Nasty Nick" Outed

In a surprise twist to the drama, viewers last night watched in astonishment as the show's cast finally woke up to the devious game being played by another character, the shadowy Nick Brown. Although he had presented himself to the others as nothing more than a nice, ineffectual gay who just wanted to get on with everyone, he was finally unmasked as a ruthless behind-the-scenes manipulator who for months has been secretly plotting to destroy British agriculture. *(Surely "be the last man left on the show"? Ed.)*

"Great news! Passes have exceeded entries this year"

News In Brief

Computer games linked to violence **3**

Pope is a Catholic **4**

Bears defecate in woods **5**

'A' Level standards have fallen **94**

Thats enough shocking new reports. Ed.)

Daily Telegraph

(formerly the Daily Hurleygraph)   Friday, August 11, 2000

Blonde Woman Takes Off Clothes

by Our Entire Staff Charles Phwoar

A TALL blonde woman today took off all her clothes in a London theatre. She stood naked for ten seconds before putting her clothes back on.

Inside

Thousands of photos and articles about the tall blonde woman, her ex-husband, their children, his love child, etc, etc, etc. *Pages 1, 2, 3, 94*. *World Copyright* The Daily Jerrygraph.

GLENDA SLAGG

The Graduate who bares all!!!

HATS AND KNICKERS off to Jerry Hall, the Leggy Lovely from the Lone Star State!!!!?! What an inspiring message to all the middle-aged mums of Britain – Get your kit off and show us what you've got!! It must make Mick rue the day he traded you in for some teenage airhead!?! Hall together now (Geddit???) Thank you Jerry Much!?!?! (Geddit??!?!)

COR BLIMEY what a sight!!?! Jerry Hall in the Hall-Together (Geddit??!?!) What does she think she looks like standin' starkers on a West End stage??!? At her age, I ask you!?!?! Even 20 seconds is far too long. I've seen a sexier frozen chicken in the ice cabinet at Tesco's, lady – no offence!?!?!

Streuth??!? No wonder Mick ditched you, and went off with a younger model!?!?! Geddit!??!?

Byeeeeeee!!?!???!

THE DAILY TELEGRAPH   FRIDAY, AUGUST 25, 2000

Letters to the Editor

Brussels bureaucracy

SIR – Your readers may be interested to know that, on a recent visit to my village's admirable watering hole, the Lamb and Flag, which for more years than I care to remember has been a stalwart bastion of all that is best about the British way of life, I was horrified to find, on purchasing a small packet of Old Ingram's Traditional Four X Pork Scratchings, that the contents of the packet were stated on the label to be "113 grams".

When I enquired of mine host, the estimable N. Balon, what was the explanation for this alien form of measurement, he informed me that the manufacturers were obliged to label their products in grams by a diktat from the faceless bureaucrats of Brussels.

What, I asked, is happening to our traditional way of life, that these mindless little Hitlers can come over here and tell us that we are no longer to measure out our pork scratchings in pounds and ounces, as we have done for centuries past?

When our ancestors fought Napoleon on the battlefields of Waterloo and Agincourt, was it not precisely to prevent the foreigner from trampling on our ancient liberties, such as the right to drink a pint of good honest English ale and measure out our cricket pitches in rods, poles and chains?

Soon no doubt we will be told that it is a criminal offence for us to go down to the pub and ask for a "double Scotch", on the grounds that some Eurocrat has issued a directive making it compulsory to drink nothing but Dubonnet in litre mugs.

It is in preparation for just such an eventuality that, with the assistance of my good friend Col. "Buffy" Frobisher, we have taken the precaution of consuming as many "doubles" as is humanly possible before the dark day when Herr Goebbels and his EU thought police came in to march us both off to the death camps.

H. GUSSETT
Furlong Cottage
Half Crown Road
Bushel Green, Dorset

PORTILLO MEETS PUPPET

THERE was a great deal of hilarity for both viewers, as Michael Portillo was confronted with his puppet on Sunday morning's edition of "Breakfast With Frost".

The puppet, known as William Hague, is a woefully unrealistic caricature of a leader of a British political party fashioned from discarded pieces of John Major and Mrs Thacher.

"He's easy to manipulate," said Mr Portillo. "All I do is apply a bit of pressure here, make him do a u-turn on tax and he has the whole country in fits of laughter."

AVOID THE FLAMING SAMBVCA

OWEN SAYS 'IT WAS ALL MY IDEA'

by Our Political Staff
Shirley Shome-Mishtake Williams

LORD OWEN sensationally claimed last night that the entire New Labour phenomenon was based on his original vision in the nineteen-eighties.

"I had it all planned out when I was running the SDP," he told reporters. "A new political party believing only in gaining power with no ideas and a smarmy figurehead who would prove ultimately disappointing."

Dr Whowen is 78.

The Robin Day I Knew

by **Lord Rees-Mogadon**

I WAS very sorry to hear of the death of my old friend Sir Robin Day, the famous broadcaster

Over the years, I have worked out that we had lunch two million times. We first met at Oxford, when we often lunched together three or four times a day. In later years, we would share a lunch table at the Garrick most days and indeed nights. I cannot recall what we used to say to each other on those happy occasions, but I have nothing but the happiest memories of our many lunches over the decades. I will miss him deeply, particularly at lunchtime. © *World copyright*.

90

"Better Late..."

A Holiday Romance Special by SYLVIE KRIN, from whose pen flowed such immortal classics as Born To Be Queen, Heir of Sorrows, and Never Too Old

"**D**O YE twa', Sarah and Gordie Brune, swear agang the Holy Buke that ye will fasten the knot betwixt ye, never to be riven asunder?"

The solemn tomes of the severe Presbyterian deaconess, the Rev. Kirsty McThirsty, rang out across the oak-panelled lounge of Drambuie Manse, the ancient granite-walled home of the Brown family.

Sarah's heart swelled with joy beneath her ivory Nomura silk wedding suit, and a perfectly-formed tear trickled down the peach-like softness of her damask cheek.

Although on the surface Sarah appeared to be a tough, abrasive career woman in the no-nonsense world of public relations, today she was just like any other young girl who has finally achieved her life's dream.

And now the great day was here at last. Not quite in the way she had dreamed of perhaps. There were no church bells chiming their message of joy to the world.

There was no pink-ribboned vintage Rolls Royce to sweep off the bridal pair to a magnificent reception attended by thousands of guests...

Still, the main thing was that she and her beloved Gordon were at last to be made one. And wasn't this simple ceremony, witnessed only by Gordon's political adviser Mr Balls, his wife Mrs Balls, and a handful of Gordie's relatives, in its own way just as moving?

"I noo pronounce ye man and wife. You may noo kiss the bride, Mr Brune."

The Chancellor of the Exchequer, his face reddening with unaccustomed embarrassment, placed a nervous kiss on his new bride's perfectly-formed damask *(Get on with it. Ed)*

"At last," thought Sarah, "at last, at last, at last..."

"**...A**t last!" exclaimed the dour Auchtermuchty Council official, Gordon's brother Hamish, "I thought the drinks would never come."

They each clutched their thimble-sized glasses of celebratory McSainsbury's champagne.

"I thought we'd have to wait six years for these wee drammies to arrive as well," joked Gordie's cousin Dougal, a much-respected accountant from the remote Highland community of Glen Campbell.

"Ha, ha, ha, ha!" Sarah joined in the laughter. After all, she could afford now to make light of the six long years she had been waiting for Gordon to pop the question she had yearned to hear. Years when Gordon had seemed more interested in abolishing the Married Person's Allowance than in becoming a married person himself.

Years when he had been more concerned with those beastly Treasury figures than in the perfectly-formed figure of his faithful fiancée.

"Raise your glasses," cried the kilted figure of Gordon's uncle Donald, a retired bank manager from the tiny Hebridean island of Isa, "and then we can let the bonnie couple gang awa' on their honeymoon..."

"**...T**he honeymoon, thought Sarah, as she came down the stairs, carrying her David Ginola travel bag. Where is Gordon taking me? He still hadn't told her.

Downstairs all the guests had departed, leaving behind only the faintest aroma from the now almost empty bottle of champagne.

It was then that she heard voices from behind the door of the adjoining kitchen. Mr Balls was talking to Gordon, excitedly.

"We've done it, Gordon, we've done it! The last piece of the jigsaw is now in place!"

She heard Gordon giving a throaty chuckle of agreement. What "jigsaw" was this? What "last piece" were they talking about?

Sarah's heart fluttered like a moth caught in a spider's web.

"You've got the economy working. Now you've given away billions to the public services. You've got Blair on the ropes. And now you've done the most difficult bit of all, you've got married.

"From now on, it's 'family man Gordon'. You'll be standing outside Number 10 clutching your own wife and kiddies' mug and your own baby Leo before you know it. So smile, Gordie. It's in the bag!"

Sarah's blood ran cold. Was that it? Just "a piece in a jigsaw..."

"Lisa, I think my wife suspects"

NAMED AND SHAMED

by Lynchtime O'Noose

THIS evil woman is responsible for an act of indescribable sickness and grotesque cynicism which must shock the entire nation. She is Rebekah Wade of Pennington Street, Wapping, a foul-minded editor psychiatrists say can never be cured of her vile tendencies.

She *will* offend again, whatever the do-gooders may say.

We publish her name only in the interests of protecting her innocent readers, many of them vulnerable morons with the mental age of a toddler. It is our duty because Rebekah Wade is not acting alone – she is part of a seedy ring of filth merchants and peddlars of pornography who are controlled by Mr Big, known only as Rupert Murdoch, who runs his evil empire from a sleazy backroom in London's criminal East End.

We strongly urge readers not to go out and string these people up, even though they would be perfectly justified in ridding the world of these sickos. No, we have plenty of rope in our office, but we urge readers *not* to come and collect their *free* hanging rope.

And although we are offering a free fortnight's holiday in sexy Ibiza for the first lynching by our readers, we strongly advise them *not* to have a go.

The Noose of the World is a responsible paper which is why we say "**Leave** justice to the forces of Law and Order – unless you don't feel they are doing a good job, in which case string up the perverts yourself."

More pictures of the faces of evil pp. 2-94.

EYE 'WRONG' TO NAME AND SHAME REBEKAH

by Our Social Affairs Staff P.D. O'Phile

THE MAGAZINE Private Eye last night came under a storm of censure for publishing a photograph of the notorious editor of the News of the World, Ms Rebekah Wade.

The police, social workers and probation officers were unanimous in their verdict that Private Eye's "naming and shaming" of Ms Wade had been "irresponsible" and "counter-productive".

String 'Er Up

A spokesman for the National Society For The Prevention of Cruelty to Tabloid Editors, the NSPCTE, said "The results of this publicity-seeking gimmick have been entirely predictable.

"Hysterical mobs of journalists have been combing London to track down this unfortunate woman and subject her to an interview.

"And now, totally predictably, this dangerous woman has gone to ground so that she can pursue her revolting activities incognito."

The Eye was also damned by Lord Longford, the veteran prison visitor, who said "I am sure Rebekah is full of contrition for what she has done. She is a very sincere Christian who needs help, not persecution by the likes of Private Eye."

Lord Longford is 106.

BLONDE WOMAN EATS CHOCOLATE AT WEDDING

Exclusive Picures Pages 1-24

On Other Pages:

Russia disintegrates	**25**
America burns	**26**
Europe in gridlock	**27**

BBC'S SECRET PLANS FOR 'FUNERAL OF THE CENTURY'

by Our Media Staff Phil Airtime

BBC boss Greg Dyke has masterminded one of the biggest projects in the Corporation's history – plans for day-long coverage of the death of Sir Reginald Kray, the well-loved King of London's East End.

Mr. David Dimbleby will head a team of 24 commentators, including his late father, who will cover the state funeral, following the cortège as it passes through the streets of the East End which were the backdrop to "Reggie's" colourful murders.

House of Windsor

Dame Barbara Windsor, the so-called "Enforcer's Sweetheart", will lead thousands of mourners in singing solemn Cockney songs, such as "Maybe it's because I'm a murderer", "Hands up Mother Brown" and "My old man said 'Kill Jack the Hat McVitie'".

Full details on Ceefax p. 861

101 Things You Can Mistake For A Paedophile

No. 1. 'Paedo-borough'

UPFRONTERS

Exclusive Pictures from the Turner/Bovey Wedding of the Millenium
The top stars turn out for Grant and Anthea's big day...

WHO'S that showbiz giant with international star clairvoyant **Mystic Meg**? Why it's TV's **Andy** from Big Brother, or is it Phil? Either way Meg, he's watching you! Talk about star gazing!?

MR. BOVEY's been granted the Turner Prize!? It's love at First Bite?! Or are they Flaking it? Anyway, **Anthea**'s the biggest star in the Milky Way and **Grant**'s the most famous man in the Galaxy! Honest!

I predict a heavy shower of **tears** from Meridian TV's star weathergirl **Trish Brightwell** (shortly to be seen on the Shopping Channel's "Celebrity Checkout" slot!!) And who is she with? Why it's **Kelly Dee**, star of the Channel 5 Docusoap "Receptionists From Hell"! Three tears for Grant and Anthea, all you celebrities!

Talk about Stars in their Eyes! Super celeb **Matthew Kelly** is toasting a bubbly blonde! And it's **Debbie** "TV's Paul Daniel's wife" **McGee** of course! Perhaps this happy couple of superstars will both disappear!!

HOW Mooo-ving! It's Emmerdale superstar **Sheree Murphy** with star Quiz Maestro **Bob Holness** and the hottest young continuity announcer on children's ITV – **Andy Simons**!? (or is it Simon Andies?) You won't forget his name in a hurry!?!

HELLO! Hello! Hello! It's Crimewatch UK's star Detective, **Inspector Bramstead** of Thames Valley C.I.D.! And who is he trying to collar – why it's Gold-Blend-TV-Coffee-Girl turned Call My Bluff panellist **Suzie Burkiss**!! Or maybe I've got that wrong and it's someone from Brookside talking to the presenter of Sky TV's Celebrity Holiday Programme "Star Treks"!? Or maybe it's GMTV's **Penny Smith** and **John Stapleton** or **Eamonn Holmes** and **Fiona Phillips**? How am I supposed to know? (*You're fired! Ed*)

WARNING: These amazing pictures are exclusive to Upfronters and any unauthorised use of these incredibly important photographs will be punished by death.

SALLY JOCKSTRAP
The Voice of Sport

SO THE Premiership has kicked off. I saw Man U at Epsom on Saturday and they were awesome.

With their new signing Tiger Woods in goal, this squad can go all the way in Sydney.

SPARE A thought for Frankie Dettori – left out of the British Lions.

If there's one man who can play table tennis, it's Sir Alex Ferguson.

No wonder we're no good at cricket. (*That's enough. Ed.*)

"You can't tackle him without going through his agent first"

WORLD'S GREATEST EVER QC RETIRES

by our Legal Staff **Joshua Rosenbeard**

THE LAST of the great legal giants has bowed out.

Last night the entire legal world was in a state of shock at the news that libel King, George Carperson, has hung up his wig and gown for the last time.

After 50 years at the bar (and almost as many in court) George Carphone is to retire, at the early age of 93.

LEADING ADVOCAAT

The news sent shock waves through the cloistered world of the Inns of Court, as tear-stained clerks and weeping barristers fought to come to terms with the prospect of a world without the man they called simply "that little bastard Carman". (surely "my learned friend"?)

Said one eminent silk, his voice trembling with emotion, "This is truly extraordinary news – perhaps now I will get some of his briefs."

Said another, "The amazing thing about George was how skilful he was at making money. We all admired and envied his incomparable genius for extracting the folding stuff from everyone he met."

The Wit and Wisdom of George Carman
Highlights of a 30 year career

On his client **Jeremy Thorpe** (1979): "Ladies and gentlemen of the jury, my client may be a homicidal poof, but since when has that been a crime?"

On his client **Ken Dodd** (1987): "OK, so my client may have fiddled the taxman out of £2 million. But which one of us has not done the same?"

On his client **Mohammed Al Fugger** (1999): "You see before you one of the finest English gentlemen it has ever been my privilege to take money from."

On his client **Richard Branson** (1999): "You see before you one of the finest English gentlemen there has ever been, apart, of course, from my good friend Mr. Fugger."

Cross-examining **David Mellor** (1994): "Mr. Mellor, I put it to you, that you are a four-eyed git."

Questioning **Miss Gillian Taylforth** (1996): "Perhaps I could give you a lift home in my Range Rover?"

Cross-examining **Mr. Neil Hamilton** (1999): "I put it to you that your only concern in life was to take money from anyone who wanted you to represent them and argue their case. Have you no shame?"

To **Mr. Alan Rubbisher**, Editor of The Grauniad: "I have pleasure in enclosing my latest fee – account totalling £2 billion, not including refreshers, and would remind you that failure to comply could lead to me acting for the other side tomorrow morning."

WHY WE MUST NEVER FORGET DIANA

by Phil Space

PRINCESS DIANA left a hole in our hearts and an even bigger hole in our newspapers.

On this, the anniversary of her tragic death, we must ensure that we do not forget to put in a huge piece regurgitating all the stuff we've already written about her.

Because if we forget to commemorate her death, we will have to think up something else to put in our newspapers.

That is why ordinary hacks like me must never, never *(continued for 94 years)*

"Hi, I'm on the make"

ESTATE AGENT

Ye Plymouth Argus

— 20 September 1619 —

Ye Voyage Of Ye Mayflower

'Damnation Upon Ye, England' Quoth Pilgrim Father

by Our Man In Plymouth **Hoe He**

A tiny band of persecuted free-thinkers yefterday set sail for ye Newe Worlde in ye good ship Mayflower, to seek a newe life in ye Americas.

Ye pafsenger liste recordeth ye following pilgrims:

Master Martin Amis, a scribe of Kensington.

Master S. Rushdie, a Moorish scribe who hath been accused of blasphemy.

Master Anthony Holden Esq., chronicler of ye royal tittle-tattle and author of *Ye Bonnie Prince Charlie I Never Knew*.

All ye pilgrims are convinced that in ye Americas their talents will at last be properly appreciated by ye local indigenous persons.

"Ye Britain is finished," quoth Mafter Holden. "It is stuck in ye Middle Ages with their out-of-date royal family, their feudal class system and their philistine obsession with ye magical feates of Mafter Harry Potter, instead of my own brilliant works such as *Ye Tchaikowsky I Never Knew* and *Ye Shakespeare I Never Knew Either*.

Added Mafter Amis, "Ye native Americans inhabit ye land of ye free. We are all fed up with Britain with its pitiful advances, carping critics and dreary women, who we are going to trade in for an American model."

YE LATE NEWS

Miftrefs Winterton, a self-confefsed witch from the county of Saffex, has alfo decided to seek a new life in ye plantations. "Perhaps ye native American critics will realise how brilliant my books are. They can't speak English, which should help."

YE EVEN LATER NEWS

An hundred thoufand Red Indians have set sail for England at the newf of the Pilgrims' arrival.

On Other Pages

How Ye New Tobacco Will Help You To Live Longer by Ye Learned Doctor Stuttaford. **2**

Why Ye Potato Will Never Catch On by Master Paul Johnson **3**

and introducing

Young Person's View: An Exciting New Column by Master Will Deedes (who is aged only 15) **4**

HAGUE SINKS 14 POINTS

by Our Other Political Staff **Bud Weiser** and **Carl S. Berg**

TORY leader William Hague yesterday claimed that he had downed a record 14 points in the course of a day and that he was "none the worse for it."

"Me and my mates decided to paint the town blue," he told the "lads'" magazine, *Tosser*. "We went round knocking on doors, and everywhere we went, we sank another two points."

"I never lost control," he went on. "I still remained in charge of the Tory Party. Indeed I could have sunk a lot more, and probably will."

William Hague is 15.

'SNATCH' PREMIERES IN WEST END

Late News

CARNIVAL RUINED

THE annual Notting Hill Murder Carnival was spoilt once again by outbreaks of dancing.

Said a police spokesman, "It is such a pity. People come here to enjoy themselves and stab each other to death and then an irresponsible minority ruins everything by going into the streets and dancing around."

He continued: "It is sad that the police have to get involved and end up doing the samba on the pavement to a calypso beat, when we would much rather be standing around watching the murdering." *(Reuters)*

"Nope, my eyesight's definitely gone"

Your Cut Out 'n' Keep Guide To The Craze That's Sweeping The Nation
Yes! It's

*

* Short for Pocket Money, Pokemon is a Japanese collecting game in which top traders Nintendo PLC collect all your children's pocket money and swap it for worthless plastic cards depicting stupid monsters. For anyone who has missed out on the fun the Eye prints a Who's Who of the top Pokemon characters.

1

PEWKACHUK – supposedly lovable and cuddly Pokemon who actually has power to make purchaser feel sick. Especially at £7.99 in a Booster Pack.

2

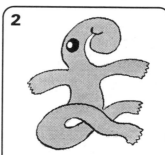

PISSAPAW – badly drawn and feeble Pokemon, PISSAPAW evolves into PIKKAFITE when older children start arguing over it. Very common.

3

FRAUDULA – even more common Pokemon due to being badly copied from the original and mass produced in China. Slightly cheaper than real Pokemon but a genuine waste of money nonetheless.

4

CHARMFREE – ill thought-out and unpleasant Pokemon and like all the others guaranteed to cost too much. Pester Power rating of 100.

5

HYPOCON –excitable marketing Pokemon who turns small coins into millions of dollars when trained by dismal Japanese computer expert with beard.

6

PSNOOZER – yet another boring, over-priced *(That's enough Pokemon. Ed.)*

GOTTA SPEND IT ALL!